Liberated for LIFE

GALATIANS

John F. MacArthur, Jr.

Regal Books

A Division of GL Publications
Ventura, CA U.S.A.

The translation of all Regal books is under the direction of GLINT. GLINT provides technical help for the adaptation, translation and publishing of books for millions of people worldwide. For information regarding translation contact: GLINT, P.O. Box 6688, Ventura, California 93006.

The Scripture quotations in *Liberated for Life* are from the *New American Standard Bible*. © The Lockman Foundation 1960, 1962, 1963, 1968, 1971, 1972, 1973, 1975. Used by permission.
Also from the *Authorized King James Version (KJV)*.

Trade edition 1984

Published by Regal Books
A Division of GL Publications
Ventura, California 93006
Printed in U.S.A.

Library of Congress Catalog Card No. 75-23511

CONTENTS

WHY DID PAUL WRITE GALATIANS?

Introduction

Magna Carta of spiritual liberty . . . Christian Declaration of Independence . . . battle cry of the Reformation . . . Charter of Freedom—all of these have been used to describe Paul's letter to the churches in Galatia.

In a way the Reformation began because Martin Luther wrote a commentary on Galatians. Out of that writing he moved to the concept of grace and faith as opposed to works, and established the protest that became Protestantism.

Luther says, "The Epistle to the Galatians is my epistle. To it I am, as it were, in wedlock. Galatians is my Katherine." To him Galatians was like a wife, so beloved was it, and his commentary became the manifesto of the Reformation.

Dr. Merrill Tenney says, "Christianity might have

been just one more Jewish sect and the thought of the western world might have been entirely pagan had Galatians never been written."

The message of Galatians is the message of liberation. It is the message of true freedom, the message of release from bondage. And Galatians is particularly relevant for today. We have all kinds of talk about liberation movements. Western man talks continuously about "freedom." He speaks about a new morality, about a new ethic. He prides himself on free speech, free right to dissent, free love, and freedom from authority. But none of it is genuine freedom. It is slavery.

Every man searches for genuine freedom. There *is* true freedom, there's no question about that. But the way to freedom is through the truth. Until man comes to the truth he is never free from his search.

Paul wrote Galatians to establish one crucial premise: spiritual freedom comes through the truth and that truth is Jesus Christ. Knowing Him is genuine freedom.

Salvation, then, is the essence of freedom. A man is a slave to sin and the struggle it causes. He comes to Christ, finds truth, and is freed from sin. The search is over. Paul says repeatedly in Galatians that Christians are free from the law of sin and the law of death.

Paul's two-fold theme in his letter to believers in Galatia is: "Let me show you how to stay free; then let me show you how to enjoy your freedom."

Now, what was it that prompted Paul to write this letter about freedom? To understand this we must take a brief look at its background.

The apostle Paul had founded some churches in southern Galatia. On his first missionary journey, which began in A.D. 47, Paul traveled several hundred miles west from Antioch of Syria to the area called Galatia. Part of what we know as Turkey today, Galatia was about 100 to 175 miles wide and about 250 miles long.

Paul took Barnabas with him and together they evangelized four primary cities: Derbe, Lystra, Iconium and Antioch of Pisidia. And in those four cities Paul established churches. After establishing those churches he turned around and traveled back through the area, strengthening the saints. Then he returned to the church in Antioch of Syria.

On his second missionary journey, beginning in A.D. 49, he took Silas with him. They went back to the same churches, and again they strengthened the believers there.

Paul had a tremendous personal love for the Galatians. They belonged to him; they were his children in the faith. But in a very short time after his second visit, the Galatian Christians had fallen prey to false teachers. They were following another gospel, and Paul was shocked.

The false teachers attacked on three fronts. First, they undermined Paul's apostolic credibility. Second, they demanded circumcision as a condition for salvation. Third, they required observation of all Jewish ceremonies and ritual.

These false teachers claimed to be Christians. Some came perhaps from the Jerusalem assembly. They may even have claimed Jerusalem's support (see Acts 15:1-5). They were called "Judaizers" for their efforts to make "Jewishness" a standard for Christianity.

In comparison to the Judaizers, Paul's teaching was clearly salvation by grace *apart from works,* and life in grace *apart from ceremony.* So in his letter to the Galatians Paul had three tasks:

- defend his apostleship and right to speak authoritatively;
- restate the gospel of grace;
- encourage Christians to live free from the law.

That is precisely what Galatians is all about. Paul defends his apostleship in chapters 1 and 2. He establishes grace as the only way of salvation in chapters 3 and 4. And in chapters 5 and 6 he shows Christians that their walk is in grace, free from the law.

In writing his letter Paul did far more than decisively refute heresy in Galatia. He wrote the Charter of Freedom for every Christian.

1
PAUL AND HIS GOSPEL

Galatians 1:1-10

No matter what the problem, Paul the apostle usually tried to start on a positive note when writing to the churches he had founded. To the Christians at Philippi he says, "I thank my God in all my remembrance of you." When writing to the church at Rome he is thankful for their faith, which is being proclaimed throughout the world. Even both letters to Corinth, the church that gave him all kinds of headaches, begin positively. And in his other letters, to Ephesus, Colossae, Thessalonica, to Timothy, Titus and Philemon, Paul starts warmly, usually with some kind of word of praise.

Galatians is the one letter Paul begins in a *much* different manner. Here he just dives right in and gets to the point—fast.

He's upset, to put it mildly, because a certain kind of thinking has been introduced by a group we will call the

"Judaizers." Paul established several churches in Galatia by preaching the gospel of grace—salvation comes through faith in Christ's substitutionary death on the cross for man's sin—*plus nothing*. The Judaizers said they "believed in Jesus as Messiah" but they added something as a requirement for salvation—circumcision, and the subsequent necessity for keeping all their ceremonies and man-made laws.

A minor operation involving the cutting and removing of the foreskin on the male penis, circumcision was a rite of high significance to Israel. Its origin can be traced back to when God made His covenant with Abraham (see Gen. 17, especially v. 11).

The Judaizers were pseudo (or false) Christians who wanted to have Christ, but keep their brand of Judaism, too. They wanted to "Judaize" the Christian faith and they were causing havoc and dissension in the Galatian churches. Their particular targets were the Gentile converts to Christ—those who came out of paganism and who were usually uncircumcised. Some Gentile converts were giving in; others were resisting, but not very strongly.

When Paul heard about what was happening in some of the very first places he had preached and established churches, he was enraged. His letter to the Galatians has been called a "flashing sword." Paul wielded that sword with fire in his eye and a conviction that came from deep within his very soul.

Paul Claims His Authority as an Apostle

Paul, an apostle (not sent from men, nor through the agency of man, but through Jesus Christ, and God the Father, who raised Him from the dead), and all the brethren who are with me, to the churches of Galatia: (Gal. 1:1,2)

As he begins his letter, Paul starts without hesitation to establish his authority. This is something that he will cover in great detail in chapters 1 and 2. He continually reminds the reader that he stands authoritatively to speak for Christ. Why? Because that was open to question in the minds of the Galatians. His right to speak as an apostle has been challenged by the Judaizers, so he introduces himself carefully.

Just identifying himself as "Paul" isn't enough. He says, "Paul, an apostle" (v. 1). Why does he emphasize that he's an apostle? Because the apostles were the ones who spoke authoritatively for Christ.

Paul wants to establish from the beginning that he is no fly-by-night, self-appointed character. His apostleship and his teaching have been questioned. The thesis of his letter to the Galatians is to answer his critics and correct the errors they have perpetrated.

When Paul calls himself an apostle, he is saying, in effect, "I have the right to speak." He uses this title in 1 Corinthians, 2 Corinthians, Romans, Ephesians and Colossians.

The term "apostle" means an envoy or delegate or ambassador. It was very familiar to the Jewish mind and referred to a special emissary, sent out with legal authority to act on behalf of the one who commissioned him. That is what an apostle was to do. "Act in my behalf," said Jesus. It was the very term that Jesus chose in Luke 6:13.

Paul did not have the benefit of being one of the Twelve. So he was self-conscious about being a true apostle and he repeatedly defends his apostleship. In 1 Corinthians 15:5,8 Paul says Peter saw the resurrected Christ, and he, Paul, also saw the resurrected Christ.

When did Paul see Him? It is recorded in Acts 9. Paul as walking down the Damascus road and was blinded. He remained blind for several days. But it was not the blindness of darkness. Rather it was the blindness of one who had seen the glory of Jesus Christ. He saw the glory of Christ and was specifically chosen. He was a legitimate apostle and he had the right to speak authoritatively for Christ. He had the same title as the Twelve—"apostle."

Paul says he is an apostle, "not . . . by man, . . . but by Jesus Christ, and God the Father . . . " (*KJV*). Paul emphasizes that his calling is not human; it is from Jesus Christ and from God. He is a *divinely* appointed apostle. Paul writes as one commissioned not by the church, but by Christ Himself.

Lastly Paul indirectly infers his authority by association. He speaks of the "brethren who are with me." He unashamedly puts himself in their company because he knows they are accepted and approved of him. The Galatians should know that other Christians have joined to support Paul's apostleship and ministry.

Thus does Paul defend his authority in order to defend his gospel.

Paul Defines His Message and Motive

Grace to you and peace from God our Father, and the Lord Jesus Christ, who gave Himself for our sins, that He might deliver us out of this present evil age, according to the will of our God and Father, to whom be the glory forevermore. Amen.
(Gal. 1:3-5)

In just two verses Paul manages to establish his message and include the whole gospel. When he writes, "grace to you and peace," he is saying something far more significant than our usual "Hi, how are you?" Grace brings peace. Grace is positional, peace is practical, and they flow from the Father through the Son.

Paul gives the gospel in verse 4 and begins with its

core—Christ's death. He points to three aspects: its nature, its purpose and its origin.

Jesus did not die a frustrated superstar. He did not die an exemplary hero for a cause. The death of Jesus Christ was not even primarily an act of love. It was a sacrifice for sin. There was love in it, but first of all it was a sacrifice. Jesus "gave Himself for our sins." He who knew no sin became sin for us (see 2 Cor. 5:21).

Then, Paul says, the purpose of Christ's death is to deliver us from this present age. If the nature of His death was sacrificial, the purpose of his death was a rescue operation. The word for deliver implies the idea of rescue. It is used in Acts 7:10 in recounting the story of Joseph. Joseph was sold into slavery but God was with him and *delivered* him out of his affliction.

Paul is saying we have been rescued from the bondage of this "present evil age." This term refers to this transitory age, the passing system operated by Satan, the system in motion, the valueless system. When we become Christians we remain in the world, but we are no longer *of* the world, no longer locked into its system.

The origin of Christ's death is in the mind of God. It was God's will that Jesus died (cf. Matt. 26:39; Acts 2:22,23). Jesus recognized that this was the Father's plan (see John 12:27-32; 18:10,11; 19:10,11). It was no accident, no foul-up of plans.

So here is the gospel. Christ gave Himself for our sins to deliver us from this present evil age, and His death is according to the will of God.

In verses 1-4, we get an introduction to Paul's message and his claim of authority. In verse 5 we see his motive—the glory of God. Paul is saying, "I am what I am, I speak what I speak, that God may be glorified." That's really what it was all about for Paul. Glorifying God by preaching the good news—the grace and peace offered to every man—was Paul's supreme purpose for living.

A Curse upon False Teachers

I am amazed that you are so quickly deserting Him who called you by the grace of Christ, for a different gospel; which is really not another; only there are some who are disturbing you, and want to distort the gospel of Christ. But even though we, or an angel from heaven, should preach to you a gospel contrary to that which we have preached to you, let him be accursed. As we have said before, so I say again now, if any man is preaching to you a gospel contrary to that which you received, let him be accursed. (Gal. 1:6-9)

Because of the magnificence of this gospel Paul is overwhelmed that the Galatians have moved in the direction of defecting from it. He is bewildered at their instability and incensed by the idea anyone could twist and pervert the gospel. Anyone tampering with the gospel—no matter who he is—will be accursed. He even says it twice for emphasis.

An understanding of cursing will give a context in which to interpret verses 6-9. Certain things have been set aside by God for cursing, for destruction. Whenever God sets something apart to be destroyed, it is *anathema*—"devoted to destruction." Throughout the history of God's dealings with men there have been certain things which God has devoted to destruction.

Let me illustrate from the life of Joshua. Moses had passed on. Joshua had taken the people into the land. They were standing before the city of Jericho when Joshua gave them this message from God: "And the city shall be accursed, even it, and all that are therein, to the Lord: only Rahab the harlot shall live, she and all that are with her in the house, because she hid the messengers that we sent. And ye, in any wise keep yourselves from the accursed thing, lest ye make yourselves accursed, when ye take of the accursed thing, and make the camp of Israel a curse, and trouble it" (Josh. 6:17,18, *KJV*).

God was cursing Jericho. He was devoting it to be destroyed. The people were to leave it to its fate. And when Achan violated God's command and took something "devoted to destruction" it cost him his life and the lives of his family (see Josh. 7:19ff.).

In the New Testament God specifically curses false teachers. A false teacher is full of deceit and mischief; he is a child of the devil, the enemy of righteousness and a perverter of the right ways of the Lord.

Keep in mind that Satan operates primarily in the area of false doctrine. Jesus simply and pointedly classified Satan as the father of lies (John 8:44). And Satan doesn't work alone; he has lying spirits that work with him—demons and fallen angels—and they usually work through *human beings*. Not only that, they usually work through *religious people*. After all, Satan is subtle. If he is going to pervert the truth, he has to get inside the truth. And that's just what he does by appearing in a very spiritual form. "Satan himself is transformed into an angel of light" (2 Cor. 11:14).

I don't think Satan spends a lot of time with bars, massage parlors, pornography or helping sell subscriptions to *Playboy* magazine. The lust of the flesh (1 John 2:16) takes care of all that quite nicely. I believe that Satan concentrates on working through false religious systems—especially within the framework of Christianity. Throughout the twentieth century he has made plenty of progress through cults, liberalism and modernism in various guises. And in recent years the occult and the Eastern religions have been extremely potent weapons in his arsenal. No matter what the package, Satan uses false teachers of religion to gain his objectives.

In the Galatian churches, the false teachers were the Judaizers. The primary objective of all false teachers is to attack the doctrine of salvation. That is the only way to obscure the truth so that the soul is kept from God. Paul's message is salvation by grace. In Galatians we see how the Judaizers had tried to spoil it with a teaching of salvation by works.

In verse 6 Paul gives a prime reason for writing this letter to the Galatians. He is shocked that so soon after he has been with them, they are deserting the gospel. The Greek word for "deserting" in verse 6 means to defect. It's the word used to refer to a turncoat. Paul is saying he can't believe it—the Galatians are already spiritual deserters. Paul blames the false teachers for their work, but he does not excuse the Galatians for going along with them so easily, giving up without a fight.

Paul says the Galatians have accepted a "different" gospel (vv. 6,7), which is really no gospel at all. The thing that was masking the deceit of the false teachers was that their gospel *sounded* like the same gospel—it had Christ dying and rising again. All they did was add works at the beginning (circumcision) and works at the end (keeping their rules) without changing the middle; and that was the subtlety of Satan. Any other gospel is no gospel at all, but a perversion of the truth.

Lastly we see Paul's warning to the false teachers. Paul says that even if it were he or an angel from heaven that were to preach any other gospel, he should be "devoted to destruction." That's *severe* language.

John later said that if a person comes to you with a false doctrine, do not let him into your house and do not bid him Godspeed (see 2 John 10,11). God warns all Christians to run from false teachers. Do not subject yourself to them in any way!

Paul Seeks to Please God, Not Man

For am I now seeking the favor of men, or of God? Or am I striving to please men? If I were still trying to please men, I would not be a bond-servant of Christ. (Gal. 1:10)

The Judaizers had probably been accusing Paul of seeking popularity. They may have been claiming he was trying to please the Gentile Christians by omitting the Jewish law. Paul responds with a flat denial.

The word "for" at the beginning of verse 10 is the Greek word *gar*. And *gar* can be used in many different ways. It could be translated "yes, indeed," "certainly," or translated as an exclamation. Perhaps the best term to use here would be "There!"

Paul asks, "There! Does that word on cursing sound like a man-pleaser?" Then he restates his commitment to Christ: "Do you think I'm going through all of this suffering and the pain and anguish in my ministry to Christ because I want to please people?"

Paul had done a lot of that suffering in Galatia and the Galatian Christians knew it. He had been stoned at Lystra and left for dead (see Acts 14:1-20).

So Paul winds up this first part of his letter by reminding the Galatians of his record. If they think about it they will realize he didn't talk like a people pleaser and he didn't act like a people pleaser. Paul's primary goal was to please God!

2
A SINGLE-MINDED MAN

Galatians 1:11-24

Paul was indeed a single-minded man. Whatever he believed, he lived it to the hilt. Looking back to his pre-Christian days, Paul (his name was Saul then) describes himself as "circumcised the eighth day, of the stock of Israel, of the tribe of Benjamin, an Hebrew of the Hebrews; as touching the law, a Pharisee" (Phil. 3:5, KJV).

Raised a traditional legalist, Paul sat at the feet of Gamaliel, master teacher among the Pharisees. Paul obeyed every minute detail of the law. We often think of Pharisees as hypocrites, but Paul was one who was not. He hid behind no mask or facade. He was totally committed to legalism—the Pharisaical concept of the law. The Pharisees were the backbone of Judaism. They loved the law, they memorized the law, they obeyed the law. And

Paul was one of the best they had.

But here, in his letter to the Galatian Christians, the dyed-in-the-wool, carefully trained legalist had nothing to offer but grace. It would take a miracle to change a man so drastically from Pharisaical legalism to the gospel of grace. But that's exactly what God did.

Paul writes Galatians—the charter of freedom—as one who knows life on both sides of the fence. After his conversion he became the champion of grace because he understood it so completely. He could see it in clear contrast to what he had known in the bondage of the law.

Only God Could Have Done It

For I would have you know, brethren, that the gospel which was preached by me is not according to man. For I neither received it from man, nor was I taught it, but I received it through a revelation of Jesus Christ. For you have heard of my former manner of life in Judaism, how I used to persecute the church of God beyond measure, and tried to destroy it; and I was advancing in Judaism beyond many of my contemporaries among my countrymen, being more extremely zealous for my ancestral traditions. (Gal. 1:11-14)

As he moves on, Paul lets his readers know the source of his gospel is superior to the message of the Judaizers. Paul's gospel is "not according to man" (v. 11). He didn't get his gospel in the way the Judaizers had gotten theirs— from the traditions of men. Paul received his message "through a revelation of Jesus Christ" (v. 12).

Paul was not an apostle of a traditional religion. He wasn't even an apostle of the Christian church. He was an apostle of the Lord Jesus Christ. God accredited him.

There's something important here, and it's the question of biblical authority. Our lives are to be subject to

Christ as He speaks through His apostles. What God says through Paul is just as authoritative as what Jesus said.

I knew a man who always carried a red-letter Bible (only the words of Jesus were printed in red). And this fellow told me, "I only believe the part in red—that's what Christ says."

How wrong he was. The part written in black by Paul, or Peter, or others, is just as important as the record of Jesus' words. It's just as important because Christ said it through them. I believe everything Paul said because Jesus Christ spoke through Paul.

Much of Judaism was based on tradition, information passed on by word of mouth. Paul is saying, "I did not receive it as you received your information—through tradition." The Jews learned under rabbinic teaching. The teacher would speak and then the student would repeat. Paul rejects entirely their usual format for learning. He says Christ Himself revealed his information to him supernaturally.

Paul knew a lot about the gospel before he was saved. He knew about Jesus Christ. He knew about the claims of Christ. But human knowledge wasn't sufficient, as evidenced by his former hatred of the gospel he now loves. Once he came to know Jesus Christ on the Damascus road, however, he was capable of receiving the supernatural truth that God would reveal to him.

In verses 13 and 14 Paul describes his preconversion attitude. There was no human way he could have come to understand grace. He hated the very concept of the gospel and persecuted Christians wherever and whenever he could.

Then, suddenly he began to preach grace. He was transformed into a man who was content to believe God and leave it at that, to accept salvation without works.

The point is, Paul's preconversion experience proves

that he did not get his message from men. No human persuasion could have changed him. Only God could turn a fanatical, legalistic ritualist into a preacher of grace. Only God could turn a persecutor of Christians into a Christian, a hater of Jesus into a lover of Jesus.

A Funny Thing Happened on the Way to Damascus

But when He who had set me apart, even from my mother's womb, and called me through His grace, was pleased to reveal His Son in me, that I might preach Him among the Gentiles, I did not immediately consult with flesh and blood, nor did I go up to Jerusalem to those who were apostles before me; but I went away to Arabia, and returned once more to Damascus. (Gal. 1:15-17)

As Paul refers to this conversion experience in verses 15 and 16, he stresses that he did not get his message from men. He was going along in pursuit of salvation by law, when it pleased God to transform him. That was the beginning. God changed him.

Paul says God "separated me from my mother's womb" (*KJV*). He is saying that from conception God separated him *to his apostleship*. Paul was chosen to be an apostle before he was born! God worked in the same way with others, including John the Baptist (see Luke 1:13-17).

God "separated" Paul—on the Damascus road—as He had planned, for a great purpose. Paul hadn't done anything to earn his salvation, nothing at all. It was purely God's grace, and God's grace literally stopped him in his tracks. There on the Damascus Road—on his way to persecute more Christians—Paul met Jesus face to face as God revealed His son in blinding glory (see Acts 9:1-21; 26:1-18).

In verse 16 the phrase, "to reveal His Son in me," is a beautiful thought. There on the Damascus road Christ was initially revealed to Paul in a glorious way. And as Paul continued to live his life, the full beauty of Christ was unfolded to him and through him. The revelation of Christ doesn't begin and end at conversion; that is only the start. Paul spent the rest of his life learning to know more about the Christ he met on the Damascus road that day when the revelation began.

In verse 16 Paul says God gave him a call to salvation and a call to service at the same time (see also Acts 26:15-18). All Christians are saved to serve. In Paul's case it was a specific kind of service and it started immediately.

Today we usually say to a new Christian, "Now that you're saved, we want to teach you before you begin to teach others." And that is normally a sound advisable procedure. But in Paul's case God did something very special and He also had something very special for Paul to do. Paul was converted, called to be an apostle and put to work—all at the same time.

When Paul says "I did not immediately consult with flesh and blood" he is claiming he had all the information he needed. His knowledge and his apostleship came directly from God. He needed no human teachers. In fact, if we look at Acts 9 (a passage that fills in the gaps of this period in Paul's life), we see that Paul preached Christ in the synagogues at Damascus *immediately after his conversion.* And from the start his preaching was so powerful and effective that he confounded the Jews (see Acts 9:19-22).

Acts 9:23 says that after "many days" had passed, the Jews wanted to kill Paul. In Greek the phrase "many days" can mean a period as long as two to three years. Putting Acts 9 with Galatians 1:17, we see that Paul apparently preached briefly in Damascus immediately after his conversion. Then he left for Arabia—not the Arabia we know today—but an area known then as Nabatean Arabia. The vast area of Nabatean Arabia included Damascus so Paul may have stayed in the general vicinity of the city.

Later Paul returned to Damascus and continued to preach there. All of this period, from conversion and initial preaching at Damascus, through the time in Arabia, and then back to Damascus, totaled three years, as indicated in verse 18.

It is interesting that when he came back, the people of Damascus began persecuting him. When Paul was in Arabia, he undoubtedly spent time in quiet introspection and a time of instruction from the Spirit. But it seems likely that he was also preaching. This may help to explain the persecution in Damascus. Second Corinthians 11:32 tells us that Aretas, King of Arabia, kept a garrison of men at Damascus. The persecution may have originated or increased because Aretas got irritated at Paul's preaching in his country during those three years.

Before God, I Lie Not!

Then three years later I went up to Jerusalem to become acquainted with Cephas, and stayed with him fifteen days. But I did not see any other of the apostles except James the Lord's brother. (Now in what I am writing to you, I assure you before God that I am not lying.) (Gal. 1:18-20)

After the three-year period in and around Damascus, Paul went to Jerusalem to meet Peter and become better "acquainted" with him (v. 18). He saw no other apostles "except James the Lord's brother" (v. 19). It is understandable that Paul wanted to get to know Peter, because Peter had been so close to Jesus. Paul could learn much about what Jesus had been like during His earthly ministry. The same was true of James—Jesus' brother—who knew as much about Jesus as Peter did, perhaps more. Paul wanted personal information about Jesus, so he spent time with Peter and James.

Note that Paul emphasizes the brevity of his visit—fifteen days. Why? He is clinching his argument for his divine appointment as an apostle. Fifteen days would have been far too short for the teaching of apostolic doctrine. Paul didn't need that kind of teaching anyway, and he needed no commissioning by the apostles. His gospel and his apostolic credentials had come directly from Christ.

In typical Jewish fashion Paul appeals to the highest court he can think of to assure the Galatians that he is telling the truth about his apostolic authority. He binds himself by saying, "Before God, I lie not" (v. 20, *KJV*). This kind of vow is *very* strong language. Any Jew saying this insincerely was inviting God's judgment and wrath.

Paul Sums Up His Argument

Then I went into the regions of Syria and Cilicia. And I was still unknown by sight to the churches of Judea which were in Christ; but only, they kept hearing, "He who once persecuted us is now preaching the faith he once tried to destroy." And they were glorifying God because of me. (Gal. 1:21-24)

Paul goes on to mention that he then went into the regions of Syria and Cilicia. That was home territory. Tarsus, where Paul had been born and reared, was in Syria. Paul stayed there for some years and founded churches. As far as we know, there were no other apostles in that area. The rest of the apostles were all down south—in Judea and Samaria.

Paul's only connection with the Christians in Judea is mentioned in verses 22-24. They had never seen him, but they heard about him and what they head caused them to "glorify God." The persecutor of the church had become a powerful preacher of the gospel. The Judean Christians recognized Paul's message as the truth and they were praising the Lord for what He had done in saving Paul.

And so Paul concludes one of the strongest arguments for apostolic authority found anywhere in Scripture. Paul claimed divine appointment as an apostle, with full authority to preach and teach the gospel. His message proved it; his conversion proved it; his record proved it; the approval of Christian leaders and laymen proved it. He had never sat under the teaching of the apostles, but he had the same knowledge and authority. Saul the single-minded Pharisee had become Paul, the single-minded apostle. God had transformed him; God had taught him; God had commissioned him; and God was getting the glory!

3
PAUL WAS PART OF THE TEAM

Galatians 2:1-10

As he opens chapter 2, Paul hastens to assure the Galatians that he is no lone superstar. He is definitely on the apostolic team. Paul does this because he had emphasized his independence of the other apostles in receiving his gospel, not from them, but directly from God. He faced the possibility of being accused of sectarianism, of preaching a gospel different from that preached by the other apostles. So he wants to demonstrate that the other apostles know him, approve of him, and accept him completely.

Paul Tells Why He Went to Jerusalem

Then after an interval of fourteen years I went up again to Jerusalem with Barnabas, taking Titus along also. And it was because of a revelation that I went up; and I submitted to them the gospel which I preach among

*the Gentiles, but I did so in private to those who were of
reputation, for fear that I might be running, or had run, in
vain. (Gal. 2:1,2)*

Paul's contacts with the apostles since his conversion
had been nil. Fourteen years after his visit to Peter he
went back to Jerusalem. In these verses, he is recalling
that experience in Jerusalem. It is obvious he didn't go
back to get his message—he had been preaching it during
the intervening fourteen years!

In verse 2 he explains why he went. God told him to
go. It seems best to identify this trip with the one
recorded in Acts 15. The circumstances in the church in
Antioch confirmed the divine directive and the church
agreed that "Paul and Barnabas and certain others of
them, should go up to Jerusalem" (Acts 15:2).

It is important to see why Paul says he went to Jerusalem "because of a revelation." He wants the Galatians to
know that he didn't go under pressure from the apostles to
get his doctrine straightened out; nor did he go because he
was at the end of his spiritual rope and couldn't understand
the truth. On the contrary, it was Paul who did the
instructing when they arrived in Jerusalem (see Acts 15:4-
11).

In Acts 15:4,5 we find that when he arrived in Jerusalem he told everybody what had been going on in their
ministry. He and Barnabas were received by the church,
the apostles and the elders and "they reported all that God
had done with them."

Apparently Paul and Barnabas met with the leaders
before they met with the congregation. Paul wanted their
strong support for the public meeting. His concern was
that all the apostles should stand together against the
Judaizers.

Paul taught the gospel of grace. It wasn't any different

from what the others had been preaching. The circumcision party (the Judaizers) had come along and claimed that a person must be circumcised to be saved. It became such a big issue that it had to be resolved.

So Paul did not come to Jerusalem to get his doctrine straightened out. He came to get the apostles to stand with him so that he would not have the Judaizers following him around and undermining everything he did. We know the apostles would not have been against Paul, but if they had been either noncommittal or soft on the legalists, his work among the Gentiles would have been "in vain."

A Living Argument Against Legalism

But not even Titus who was with me, though he was a Greek, was compelled to be circumcised. But it was because of the false brethren who had sneaked in to spy out our liberty which we have in Christ Jesus, in order to bring us into bondage. But we did not yield in subjection to them for even an hour, so that the truth of the gospel might remain with you. But from those who were of high reputation (what they were makes no difference to me; God shows no partiality)—well, those who were of reputation contributed nothing to me. (Gal. 2:3-6)

Titus, a saved, converted, uncircumcised Gentile, went with Paul to Jerusalem. It is amazing how the presence of one uncircumcised, saved Gentile adds weight to the argument. If anyone were going to say one had to be circumcised to be saved, he would have to talk Titus out of his salvation.

The Judaizers were claiming that the apostles and the church at Jerusalem were insisting that a man had to be circumcised to be saved. So Titus was something of a test case, and grace won instead of ceremonial law.

The Judaizers were looking to Jerusalem for support,

but they didn't get it. The apostles did not require Titus to be circumcised when he was with them in Jerusalem, and Paul is careful to let the Galatians know it. If the apostles in the home church at Jerusalem did not require circumcision of Gentiles, how could the non-apostolic Judaizers require it of Gentiles *outside* Jerusalem?

Paul won a great victory there in Jerusalem, but it didn't come easily because there were Judaizers present in the meeting. Paul calls them "false brethren" (v. 4). The *New English Bible* translates it "sham-Christians" and Phillips calls them "pseudo-Christians." Both are very accurate definitions. These false brethren were not true believers. They were legalists, trying to earn their salvation, and they had eliminated grace (see Gal. 5:2).

Verse 4 says these false brethren "sneaked in to spy out our liberty." By this Paul means the Judaizers were trying to find weak points in the gospel, weaknesses in the liberty provided by Christ.

Jesus said that if the Son makes you free, you are free indeed (see John 8:36). The Judaizers who had sneaked into the Jerusalem conference hoped to find some contradictions, some loopholes somewhere so they could undermine and discredit the gospel of grace and prove their way was best.

But they failed. They failed because liberty in Christ was so solid, so much better than legalism. In Christ there is freedom from law as a way to God. In Christ there is freedom from sin's penalty and the curse of the law, which is death. In Christ there is freedom from the external ceremonies that the law demands.

Jesus had come to men and said, "You've got a problem and it's *you*. Let me set you free from you." To be free from yourself—that is to be free indeed and Paul knew it. That's why the Judaizers' spying did them no good.

The unyielding stance of Paul and Barnabas and their

strong support by the Jerusalem apostles and leaders were to show the Judaizers that the prominent leaders of the Jerusalem church agreed with Paul's grace message.

For 17 years Paul had been preaching his message independent from the Jerusalem church. When he came to Jerusalem, its great leaders—"those of high reputation"—could contribute nothing to him (v. 6). They had never taught him, and now did not have a single thing to add to what Paul already knew. He was a full-fledged member of the apostolic team, with equal credentials and authority.

Paul Commissioned, Commended and Reminded

But on the contrary, seeing that I had been entrusted with the gospel to the uncircumcised, just as Peter with the gospel to the circumcised (for He who effectually worked for Peter in his apostleship to the circumcised effectually worked for me also to the Gentiles), and recognizing the grace that had been given to me, James and Cephas and John, who were reputed to be pillars, gave to me and Barnabas the right hand of fellowship, that we might go to the Gentiles, and they to the circumcised. They only asked us to remember the poor—the very thing I also was eager to do. (Gal. 2:7-10)

In verse 7 Paul talks about the "gospel of the uncircumcision" and the "gospel of the circumcision." Is Paul referring here to two different gospels? The Greek form used is what we call an objective genitive, in which the noun in the genitive case receives the action. It should read, "The gospel *to* the uncircumcision was committed unto me and the gospel *to* the circumcision unto Peter." The gospel remained the same; the assignments were different—Paul to the Gentiles, Peter to the Jews.

Paul makes a dramatic claim in verse 8. He says the

same Holy Spirit empowered him and Peter to preach the same message. Both their ministries were authenticated and confirmed by God. And in verse 9 we see that the "pillars of the church"—Peter (Cephas), James and John—recognized God's grace and power at work in Paul. They gave Paul, and Barnabas, "the right hand of fellowship." Nowadays we shake hands with everybody; it doesn't mean anything. But in those days the right handclasp was the sign of promise and trust and friendship. It was the right hand of *koinonia*.

The personal noun from *koinonia* is the word we translate "partner." James, Peter and John, the pillars of the Jerusalem church, accepted Paul as a "partner"! And if Paul's gospel was accepted, it was obvious his apostleship was accepted also.

Imagine what the Judaizers must have thought when they read that the Jerusalem apostles took Paul's hand and said, "We are partners." It was all over for the Judaizers.

Verse 10 contains a brief phrase that is loaded with significance. Satisfied with Paul's doctrine and calling, the Jerusalem church asked him to "remember the poor."

The church in Jerusalem faced a very difficult situation. There were tremendous numbers of poor people in the city, including many pilgrims who had scraped together everything they had to come to Jerusalem. Some of these people had been saved while they were there and did not want to return home. They wanted to stay with the Christian community, but they had no means of support in the city. Funds had to be forthcoming from other sources to provide for them. In typical fashion, Paul was more than happy to help. For Paul, sound doctrine always led to practical Christian love and concern. Throughout his missionary career, Paul constantly wrote and worked to help the poor (see 1 Cor. 16; 2 Cor. 9; Rom. 15).

This brief thought about "remembering the poor" is for

us also. Many who identify with the fundamental end of the Christian scale sometimes tend to shy away from responsibilities to the poor. We get so busy, so involved in our own concerns, that we are unaware and uncaring in cases where people have real needs. But doctrine should always lead to action. If we refuse to show compassion to those in need, we deny the doctrine we say we so firmly believe.

So, in Galatians 2:1-10 we see Paul looking back on a key event in his life—a "showdown" with the Judaizers before the apostolic leaders of the church at Jerusalem (recorded in Acts 15). In this passage we learn something of Paul and the conflicts he faced. We see the authority of the apostles and how Paul shared fully in that authority. We see that the gospel of grace is to be defended to the fullest.

Finally we get a beautiful picture of New Testament unity—not the theology of Paul, not the theology of Peter, not the theology of John or James, but the *theology of God,* represented by all these men.

4
NOT PAUL, BUT CHRIST

Galatians 2:11-21

As he looked back on his conversion and early years of Christian service, Paul listed his *apostolic credentials* (Gal. 1:1-24). Then he went on to recall the showdown with the Judaizers at Jerusalem and how he received *apostolic commendation* from the top leaders of the church (Gal. 2:1-10).

In this next passage we find him describing his *apostolic confidence*. Here we see Paul in a dramatic defense of his apostleship, as he recalls a conflict with Peter. Paul won the argument and showed superior authority over the man thought to be the most prominent of all apostles.

Paul Clashes with Peter

But when Cephas came to Antioch, I opposed him to his face, because he stood condemned. For prior to the

*coming of certain men from James, he used to eat with the
Gentiles; but when they came, he began to withdraw and
hold himself aloof, fearing the party of the circumcision.
And the rest of the Jews joined him in hypocrisy, with the
result that even Barnabas was carried away by their
hypocrisy. But when I saw that they were not
straightforward about the truth of the gospel, I said to
Cephas in the presence of all, "If you, being a Jew, live like
the Gentiles and not like the Jews, how is it that you compel
the Gentiles to live like Jews?" (Gal. 2:11-14)*

Both Peter and Paul were Christians; both were apostles; both were honored by the church; both were vested
with authority by Jesus Christ Himself. Yet, here they are
in a head-to-head confrontation.

Notice the word "opposed," which Paul uses in verse
11. It means to set oneself against. It usually applies when
the initial attack comes from another source and you set
yourself in defense.

In Paul's eyes, Peter was *attacking* the gospel of
grace, by what he was doing. Actually, it was a case of
what Peter was *not* doing and Paul recounts the incident
here as a defense of his authority. After his experience at
Simon's house in Joppa (see Acts 10) Peter had begun eating (fellowshipping) with Gentile Christians. In Galatians
2:12 the Greek for "used to eat" is an imperfect tense of
the verb, which means continuous action. Peter had been
in the habit of eating with Gentiles. He understood the
plan of God for the church (see Mark 7:19; Acts 10:9-18).

Formerly Jews had never eaten with Gentiles. The
Old Testament rules regarding clean and unclean food forbade it. And the man-made restrictions handed down from
generation to generation by the rabbis made it impossible.
In fact, a Jew who ate with Gentiles was considered
wicked. But Christ had abolished all this. The wall of sepa-

ration was down. The church was one; the love feast and communion were for all. Peter knew this. When he first arrived in Antioch he fell right in line with this unity. They were all brothers.

James, the leader of the Jerusalem church and the brother of our Lord, was a godly man and would not be one to create chaos where harmony existed. Yet certain men came to Antioch claiming to have been sent by James. But in fact they were Judaizers, only professing to be Christians from Jerusalem (see v. 12).

These visitors were "of the circumcision," Judaizers who wanted to impose their legal system. It was these men whose arguments and demands James rejected at the council in Jerusalem (see Acts 15:19). But when they had come to Antioch with their demand that Jews not eat with Gentiles they somehow managed to intimidate Peter. He had withdrawn and separated himself from Gentile believers, even though he knew the Judaizers were wrong. Peter stood condemned by his own actions.

It's not hard to condemn yourself by what you do. For example, I could go to an art museum, see a renowned masterpiece, and say, "It stinks, it's terrible." But I do not condemn the painting, I condemn myself, because I obviously don't know art.

Or, I can go hear a great symphony played by a great orchestra, come out of the hall and say, "What lousy music." Again, I condemn myself, because I obviously don't know good music. My actions prove it.

In this same way Peter's actions had condemned him. He had withdrawn, probably with lame excuses about why he could not eat with the Gentile Christians.

The word "withdraw" (v. 12) is the Greek word used to describe a strategic military maneuver. Expressed in the imperfect tense, the word suggests a gradual withdrawal.

The term "hold himself aloof" is also in the imperfect and implies a gradual separation. Peter had just stopped accepting invitations from Gentiles and quietly faded out.

What did Peter fear? He didn't want to antagonize these men and have them give a bad report on him to their like-minded friends in Jerusalem. Peter was apparently trying to protect his prestige and popularity among the Jews.

Paul sees Peter's behavior as a serious attack on the gospel of grace. Peter was playing right into the hands of the Judaizers by refusing to eat (including probably a meal, the love feast and communion) with Gentile Christians. The fact that the Lord's table was involved made it all the more serious, for it is the sacrament of unity (see 1 Cor. 10:17).

There are some people today who want to have a separate communion for the super-holy or the super-separated, but what they do is exactly what Peter did. This kind of disunity gives the world a distorted picture of the Body of Christ.

A drastic consequence of Peter's deviation was that the rest of the Jewish Christians at the Antioch church pulled out with him. The word "hypocrisy" means to conceal one's real character.

The Greek word literally says "to answer from under" and was often used to refer to Greek actors, who wore masks as they presented plays. The actors spoke from under the masks. From this background comes the word "hypocrite"—someone who masks his real ideas or feelings (i.e., a phony).

Even Barnabas was carried away with the hypocrisy (see v. 13). That was the final blow. Barnabas, one of their own pastors, helped split the church right down the middle. What a terrible, tragic thing was happening to the loving oneness of the Antioch church. They were all falling into the hypocrisy of legalism.

Even great ministers of the gospel can make serious mistakes. God's Word may be infallible but His people are not. This is a warning against ever giving to any human being the robe of infallibility. We learn from Peter that it is not enough to believe the gospel—*you must be willing to obey it.*

Paul was fighting for the purity of the church as well as contending for the truth of grace, salvation and liberty. When he says in verse 14 that Peter and the others "were not straightforward about the truth of the gospel," he uses a Greek word meaning they did not walk "with straight feet." They did not stay parallel to the truth. Peter knew the truth and believed it. Peter believed he could eat with the Gentiles. That was clear from the record of Acts 10. Now he was denying by his behavior what he knew to be true.

So Paul brings the problem of Peter's hypocrisy before them all. Augustine once said that it is not advantageous to correct in secret an error which occurred publicly. Augustine was right. Public sin must be dealt with on a public basis (see Matt. 18:17; 1 Tim. 5:20). Credibility has to be established on the basis of action. If we preach holiness and godliness and purity and do not enact discipline, people are going to think we don't mean what we say. In this case Paul sets a courageous example for the church. He publicly unmasks hypocrisy in one who is an important individual in the eyes of the people.

In verse 14 Paul says in effect to Peter: "You gave up the Jewish laws and have been living like a Gentile. Now you suddenly seem to want to go back to the old system and make the Gentiles live like the Jews!"

What Does It Mean to Be Justified?

We are Jews by nature, and not sinners from among the

*Gentiles; nevertheless knowing that a man is not justified
by the works of the Law but through faith in Christ Jesus,
even we have believed in Christ Jesus, that we may be
justified by faith in Christ, and not by the works of the
Law; since by the works of the Law shall no flesh be
justified. (Gal. 2:15,16)*

Verse 15 continues the speech that Paul made to Peter
as he rebuked him for violating the cardinal doctrine of
Christianity—justification by faith. He points out that
"we" (he and Peter) are Jews by birth, not mere Gentile
sinners. *Nevertheless,* even the Jews have been given a
wonderful revelation. The only way to be saved is through
faith in the Lord Jesus Christ.

The Judaizers were willing to "have faith" but they also
insisted you had to work at it. *If* you keep the commandments . . . *if* you are circumcised . . . *if* you accept Judaism . . . and *if* you fast and pray and give your alms—IF
you do all these things, you will make the grade and you
will be justified by the works of the law.

Three times in verse 16 Paul emphasizes God's way is
by faith in Jesus Christ, not the law. The first statement is
general: "A man is not justified by the works of the Law,
but through faith in Christ Jesus . . . . " *Every* man must
come to God the same way—through justification by faith.

The second statement is personal: "Even we have
believed in Christ Jesus, that we may be justified by faith
in Christ, and not by the works of the Law . . . . " *Even
Peter and Paul,* with all their advantages in being Jewish
and knowing the Law, had to come through justification by
faith.

The third statement is universal: "By the works of the
Law shall no flesh be justified." Here Paul quotes from
Psalm 143:2. The Greek word for "flesh" is a strong term,
referring to *all mankind* without exception.

Every generation has been asking in its own way the very same question that Bildad asked centuries ago in Job 25:4, "How then can man be justified with God?" *(KJV)*. It is a *very* important question.

One of the universal human hurts is guilt. Every man feels it; every man tries in some way or another to alleviate his guilt. He may salve it over with self-confidence and positive thinking, or he may endeavor to escape from it in drugs or drink or some other refuge. But everyone tries in one way or another to deal with guilt.

The primitive man may attempt to pacify some god he thinks exists. The cultured man perhaps looks for a way out through psychoanalysis. But those at both ends of the scale, whether cultured or primitive, shout that something is still wrong. They need love! They need acceptance! They need forgiveness!

And it is at that point that the good news of the gospel of Jesus Christ rings true. The voice of God says there is love, there is acceptance and there is forgiveness—for all who come to God through Jesus Christ.

This is the core of the Scripture and speaks to the human dilemma: "God is righteous and I am sinful. How do I get to God?" Peter was adulterating and prostituting the fact that man is brought to God by faith in Jesus Christ alone. Paul was counterattacking this; his words became a presentation of the doctrine of justification.

"Dead" to the Law . . . "Alive" in Christ

But if, while seeking to be justified in Christ, we ourselves have also been found sinners, is Christ then a minister of sin? May it never be! For if I rebuild what I have once destroyed, I prove myself to be a transgressor. For through the Law I died to the Law, that I might live to God. I have been crucified with Christ; and it is no longer I who live, but Christ lives in me; and the life which I now

*live in the flesh I live by faith in the Son of God, who loved
me, and delivered Himself up for me. I do not nullify the
grace of God; for if righteousness comes through the Law,
then Christ died needlessly. (Gal. 2:17-21)*

It is difficult to untangle verses 17—21. Paul is still fir-
ing away at the inconsistency of Peter and Barnabas, and
in verse 17 he jabs hard at a key issue. Christ wanted Jew
and Gentile to be one—no more division or separation.
But Peter, through separating himself from the Gentiles,
was agreeing with the Judaizers that unity between Jew
and Gentile was sinful. This, says Paul, is tantamount to
saying Christ is the minister of sin!

Paul ends verse 17 with the strongest possible negative in the Greek. "May it never be!" is equal to, "God forbid!" In verse 18 Paul says he would prove *himself*, not
Christ, to be the sinner if he forsook the law, accepted
grace, and then turned back to the law. The fact that the
Judaizers were holding on to law makes them the sinners.
Paul cannot go back. The very thought clashes head on
with his deep conviction that he has "died to the Law" (v.
19).

What does this mean? Paul says he has come to grace;
he was come to God through faith; he cannot go back to a
system of legalism. If ever any man could have been saved
by strict obedience to the law, it might have been Paul.
But he says in verse 19 that all he got from knowing the
law was death. All the law did for him was enable him to
know he couldn't keep it! Then the law "killed" him.

In his letter to the Romans Paul expands on this same
idea. He says, "The wages of sin is death" (Rom. 6:23).
"Since I am a sinner I am going to have to die." Then in
Romans 7:1 he tells how the law has dominion over a man
as long as he lives, but once he has died, the law no longer
has any claim on him.

We can illustrate what Paul is saying in this way: suppose you commit a capital crime. The law convicts you and has the right to kill you—once. Suppose they put you in the gas chamber and release the gas. After the gas clears away the executioner opens the door and unstraps you. Just at that moment you return to life, rub your eyes, and exclaim that it's good to be alive again. The executioner faints and you walk out of there with the law having no further claim on you. Paul's point is this: as long as you live, the law has a claim on you. But when you die, the law's claim is cancelled. If you come alive after that death, the law can make no claim on you.

That's why Paul goes on to say he has been "crucified with Christ" (v. 20). Paul is saying that in a spiritual sense, when Christ died on that cross, he (Paul) died too. Paul was there spiritually when Christ paid the penalty for his sin. And, in a spiritual sense, Paul "came alive" in Christ by placing his faith in Him.

The verb "crucified" is in the perfect tense, which means a past completed action with present results. Paul has been crucified with Christ and the result is still producing benefits. It is no longer Paul who lives; Christ lives in Paul; and what happened to Paul has happened to every Christian. What an incredible reality! Christ alive in me— living His divine life through me! No wonder Paul said in Ephesians 3:20 that Christ does exceeding abundantly above all we ask or think "according to the power that works within us." No wonder Peter said that we are partakers of His divine nature (see 1 Pet. 1:4).

Even though I have been "crucified with Christ," I'm still alive, and the life I now live in this body has been transformed through faith—faith in the Son of God who loved me and died for me! As Paul said in Colossians 1:27, Christ lives in me and is my hope of glory!

I don't need to work and struggle to get near God. I

know where God is; He's inside—me. It's only a question of yielding to His presence.

In verse 21, Paul concludes his speech by realizing his righteousness is a gift. He did not earn it; he simply accepted it. If he tried to earn it, he would be nullifying (or canceling out) God's grace. Paul is saying, "I'll never go back to the law. If I do that, I admit that righteousness comes by the law, and if that's true, Christ died in vain."

The two pillars of the Christian faith are the grace of God and the death of Christ. The grace of God was always there, but the death of Christ made it something we could receive. If anybody insists that he can earn salvation by his own efforts, he undermines the very foundations of Christianity. He nullifies the cross.

Martin Luther, champion of the Reformation, was a perfect example of discipline, a perfect example of penance, a perfect example of self-denial to the point of self-torture.

Martin Luther tried it all: flagellating himself with whips, climbing many flights of rough stone steps on his bleeding hands and knees. He toiled to take years off his sentence to purgatory. He toiled to win merit. He worked and slaved for his justification but nothing helped. He came to despair and it was then that God stepped in, with one verse of Scripture: "The just shall live by faith" (Rom. 1:17, *KJV*). Martin Luther believed and the walls of legalism came crashing down. He became crucified with Christ, yet he lived and Christ lived in him to do a work that changed the world.

5
THE CASE FOR GRACE

Galatians 3:1-18

Having established his apostolic credentials and authority, Paul now moves into the doctrinal section of his letter. Here Paul will fully answer the Judaizers who have condemned salvation by grace through faith alone. He will defend the doctrine of justification by faith from the standpoint of experience and from the standpoint of Scripture.

In this next passage Paul will have much to say to people who don't take advantage of the opportunity to learn the truth. This is very significant for us today. Our faith ought to be established, not in our emotions, but in our minds. The emotional response will follow.

In Ephesians 4:23 Paul wrote, "Be renewed in the spirit of your *mind*" (italics mine). Many people who profess Christ as Saviour by faith get sidetracked into legalistic systems because they fail to use their brains to examine Scripture and to think things through. They listen to the so-called experts whom Satan uses to play on their emotions. The study of the Word of God is a great protection against false doctrine because it roots you in the truth.

Paul Makes a Case from Experience

You foolish Galatians, who has bewitched you, before whose eyes Jesus Christ was publicly portrayed as crucified? This is the only thing I want to find out from you: Did you receive the Spirit by the works of the Law, or by hearing with faith? Are you so foolish? Having begun by the Spirit, are you now being perfected by the flesh? Did you suffer so many things in vain—if indeed it was in vain? Does He then who provides you with the Spirit and works miracles among you, do it by the works of the Law, or by hearing with faith? (Gal. 3:1-5)

When Paul says, "You foolish Galatians," it is probably a combination of anger and love mixed with amazement. The Greek word for "foolish" literally means, "You who do not think." Phillips translates it "You dear idiots." Paul is not talking about the absence of intelligence; he is talking about the failure to use it! To use a more contemporary expression, the Galatians were acting like blockheads.

The Galatians were blockheads for listening to the legalistic pitch of the Judaizers, because they just didn't think it through. They didn't think it through in the light of Scripture. They let the Judaizers convince them with a clever sales talk, flavored with a lot of "sincerity."

The Galatians are a vivid illustration of how people get lured into cults and false doctrines today. They follow their feelings. They follow their hearts, their fantasies, their whims—*they don't think it through*. They don't study the Scripture for themselves and make real comparisons.

They just swallow a smooth line of heresy because, "Well, they were such wonderful people and . . . oh, it all seemed so good."

But when you buy a smooth line of heresy, there is always a hook on the end of it. Total misinformation and total untruth—if presented with the right salesmanship and emotional pitch—can stir you up to make wrong decisions and do stupid things. Hitler knew this. So do some advertisers and politicians. So do playboy types with fast cars and fast hands.

You can respond emotionally to lies as well as you can to truth, but when your mind is confirmed in truth, you can be immovable. Follow your head, not your feelings.

In the last phrase of verse 1 Paul talks of Christ being publicly portrayed as "crucified." He is saying here that the Galatians have openly seen the gospel presented in the crucified Christ. Paul himself first preached Christ to the Galatians. So vividly had he presented Christ to the Galatians that they could *see* Him crucified. They were convicted of their sins, they repented, they accepted His perfect sacrifice, they forsook their sin and their paganism, and by faith they entered the Kingdom.

The word used for crucified in the Greek is a perfect passive participle. This form expresses an historical fact with continuing results. Christ was crucified in history, but at the moment that anybody believes in Jesus Christ, he is crucified with Christ. The crucifixion of Christ in a sense continues to go on. The cross is an historic fact with continuing results. The cross continues to be that which substitutes for sin. Once you believe in Christ, you can't move in with some additional religious ritual to "pick up where the cross leaves off." The cross never leaves off. It stands forever, as living proof that men cannot redeem themselves (see also Acts 13:39).

In verse 2 Paul asks how the Galatians received the

Holy Spirit. They didn't have to do any spiritual gymnastics to receive Him. They simply believed. The gift of the Holy Spirit is the most unmistakable evidence of God's favor there is. The Spirit witnesses that we are the children of God (see Rom. 8:16,17). When God gives His Spirit, He gives Him only to those who believe. When a person comes to Christ, God gives the Spirit as evidence of His acceptance and as the absolute guarantee of eternal salvation.

In Ephesians 1:13,14, Paul says the Holy Spirit is given as a "pledge of our inheritance" in Christ. The Greek word used for "pledge" means a down payment or first installment. It was also used to refer to an engagement ring. When you get saved God says, "I have an inheritance for you and I'll give you a guarantee, an engagement ring—the Holy Spirit." Every Christian can say he's going to the marriage supper of the Lamb someday because he knows he is part of the bride of Christ (see Rev. 19:7-9). He has the Holy Spirit; he has an engagement ring.

Paul asks the Galatians, "Did you need legalism to know Christ? Did you need legalism to receive the Holy Spirit? Use your heads!" The answer is obvious; they had received the Holy Spirit by believing in the Lord Jesus Christ. The law could not give the Holy Spirit. The Spirit is procured by faith in Jesus Christ. The Holy Spirit is not the *goal* of the Christian—the Holy Spirit is the *source* of the Christian life.

In verse 3 Paul again calls the Galatians "foolish." A bit satirically he asks, "After starting right with the Spirit, have you decided you can do a better job on your own?"

It's important here to differentiate between trusting in works for salvation and trusting in Christ for salvation, which then leads to good works. The law says: do this and you will live. The New Testament says: you live, so do this. Good works are a verification of our salvation (see Jas. 2:14).

When we talk about good works today, we usually think of good deeds: helping people, contributing money to worthy causes—specific arts of moral decency. The Judaizers, however, weren't even talking about moral acts. They were counting on works of the law done through ceremonies like circumcision.

In verse 4 the word "suffer" is a neutral term that can be better translated "experience." This is the key to this whole passage. Paul is saying, "Haven't your experiences taught you anything?" The Galatians had experienced salvation through Christ and they had experienced the fullness of the gift of the Holy Spirit. Was it all needless?

Verse 5 mentions the One who provided the Spirit and who worked miracles among the Galatians—God the Father. The word "provides" means to supply bountifully. The Greek word has an interesting background. In classic Greek writings we find the same word used to describe a person who would pay for a chorus to provide background in a play—a very expensive proposition.

The same word was common in marriage contracts during Paul's time. It referred to the support that a husband, out of love, promised to give his wife.

This word then has to do with benevolent support, benevolent giving. And here in Galatians 3:5 it speaks of the benevolent giving of God who ministers to the believer out of love.

Paul Clinches His Case with Scripture

Even so Abraham believed God, and it was reckoned to him as righteousness. Therefore, be sure that it is those who are of faith that are sons of Abraham. And the Scripture, foreseeing that God would justify the Gentiles by faith, preached the gospel beforehand to Abraham, saying,

*"All the nations shall be blessed in you." So then those who
are of faith are blessed with Abraham, the believer. For as
many as are of the works of the Law are under a curse; for
it is written, "Cursed is every one who does not abide by all
things written in the book of the Law, to perform them."
Now that no one is justified by the Law before God is
evident; for, "The righteous man shall live by faith."
However, the Law is not of faith; on the contrary, "He who
practices them shall live by them." (Gal. 3:6-12)*

Beginning with verse 6, Paul turns to an even higher
authority to prove his argument—Scripture. The only
Scripture available to Paul was the Old Testament, and he
uses it as the supreme defense of salvation by faith.

This is important, because there are many people who
think the Old Testament teaches salvation by works. But
God is consistent; *salvation is always by faith, never by
works of righteousness.*

Of course, people in Old Testament times were not
required to believe in the death, resurrection and second
coming of Christ. They had to believe as much as God had
revealed to that point in time. A man was required to
believe all that God said. But in Old Testament times you
couldn't *make* yourself any more righteous than you can
today.

In verses 6-9 Paul refers to Scripture to present *positive proof* of justification by faith, not works. God came to
Abraham and asked him to move far away to an unknown
destination (see Gen. 12). Abraham was 75 at the time;
old people have their roots down deep. But Abraham
believed God and was justified (see Gen. 15:6). Later, he
was circumcised as a sign of his covenant with God.

The Judaizers tried to use Abraham's circumcision to
their advantage. They were urging the Galatians to be circumcised as Abraham had been, to gain the ultimate sign

of salvation. Paul knew this, *but* Paul also knew that Abraham had not been circumcised until *14 years after* being declared righteous in God's sight (compare Gen. 15:1-6 with Gen. 17:24-26). Abraham submitted to the physical sign of circumcision, not to be justified before God, but to demonstrate God's covenant and the separation between Israel and pagan tribes around them (see Gen. 17:10-14).

So, Paul emphasizes that Abraham *believed God* and was declared righteous (v. 6). Only those who have real faith (not outward signs of ceremony) are true sons of Abraham (v. 7).

The Judaizers were also using a fallacy by pointing to Abraham as a key example of why you have to keep the law to be saved. The law came from God, through Moses, but Abraham lived many centuries *before* Moses. There was no law in Abraham's day. God saved (justified) Abraham by *faith,* not by obedience to the law.

Had the Judaizers "done their homework" on Abraham they would have seen the weakness in their whole argument. The act of circumcision, as a sign of earthly covenant, did not change, or improve, Abraham's status. Abraham was justified by faith, years before being circumcised, and centuries before the giving of the law. The circumcised person is not automatically saved. Circumcision is a sign of an earthly identity; salvation, of a heavenly identity.

Abraham's salvation was granted to him by faith, and his life is an illustration of the manner in which men in all ages are saved. He is the supreme example that salvation is spiritual, internal, personal, *by faith.* He is in that sense the father of all people who come to God by faith. This is not on the basis of race, but of spiritual oneness. Being of Jewish descent doesn't guarantee anything. Those who do not come by faith alone are *not* Abraham's spiritual children.

Verse 8 reveals that at the very time that Abraham

was given the promise, God told him the Gentile nations would be saved by faith. They would not have to become Jews. The Bible does not say, "And all the nations shall become what you are." Genesis 12:3 says, "And in you all the families of the earth shall be blessed." So, then, says Paul, to sum up his argument with positive proof from Scripture, all those who depend on justification by faith (without works) are placed with Abraham, the *believer.* All are objects of God's blessing.

In verse 10 Paul switches gears to use Old Testament Scripture as *negative proof* of justification by faith.

Paul turns the tables on the Judaizers by using Deuteronomy 27:26 to show that the law does not justify anybody and anybody depending on the law for salvation is under a curse. Anybody trying to live under legalism binds himself to live by the *whole* law and that is impossible. That person is cursed by permanent alienation from God.

In verse 11 Paul goes again to the Old Testament to point out, "The righteous will live by his faith" (Hab. 2:4). And in verse 12 he uses the Old Testament to give fair warning to those who want to trust in the law for salvation. He refers to Leviticus 18:5 when he says, "He who practices them [the laws] shall live by them." If we decide we want to trust the law for salvation, then we have to live by it to the letter—perfect performance. One mistake and we have had it.

It is as if a ship were moored, held by a strong chain, to some great solid rock. But then a tremendous storm comes up. Only one link need be broken, and the ship will be lost.

Paul destroys any hope in the law by saying that law and faith are opposite and mutually exclusive. *They cannot go together.*

Christ Was Cursed to Keep God's Promise

Christ redeemed us from the curse of the Law, having become a curse for us—for it is written, "Cursed is every one who hangs on a tree"—in order that in Christ Jesus the blessing of Abraham might come to the Gentiles, so that we might receive the promise of the Spirit through faith. Brethren, I speak in terms of human relations; even though it is only a man's covenant, yet when it has been ratified, no one sets it aside or adds conditions to it. Now the promises were spoken to Abraham and to his seed. He does not say, "And to seeds," as referring to many, but rather to one, "And to your seed," that is, Christ. What I am saying is this: the Law, which came four hundred and thirty years later, does not invalidate a covenant previously ratified by God, so as to nullify the promise. For if the inheritance is based on law, it is no longer based on a promise; but God has granted it to Abraham by means of a promise. (Gal. 3:13-18)

In verse 13, Paul offers the glorious remedy to end the desperation of people trying to live by the law. Christ removed the curse of the law by "becoming a curse for us."

What does Paul mean? He refers again to the Old Testament: "Cursed is every one who hangs on a tree" (see Deut. 21:23). According to Jewish law, every criminal sentenced to death was to be executed, usually by stoning. Then his body would be taken and tied to a post or "hanged on a tree." This was a visible symbol of his rejection—something people could see. The criminal was not cursed by God because he was hanged on a tree; he was hanged on a tree because he was cursed by God.

It is no wonder the Jews would not believe Jesus was their Messiah. They knew Jesus died on a cross, that He was "hanged on a tree." But how could the Messiah be cursed by God? The Jews could not grasp one vital point: Christ was not "cursed" because of His own sin. He was cursed because He bore man's sin in His own body, and God cannot look on iniquity.

We all deserved the curse, but Christ took it for us. If you cannot keep the law, you are cursed. But God comes and says you do not have to bear your own curse. God substituted His Son in your place. Jesus took *your* curse, died *your* death, paid *your* penalty.

Through Christ sin has been dealt its death blow. It is all part of God's plan to fulfill His purpose. He wants all men to be made righteous and receive what was promised to Abraham—"the promise of the Spirit through faith" (v. 14).

In verses 15-18 Paul nails down the superiority of God's promise to Abraham over the demands of the law. God gave Abraham a promise with no conditions. From Abraham's loins would come the seed that would bless all men.

To understand verse 15 we have to turn to Genesis 15 to learn how a covenant was made and confirmed. Abram questioned God because he had no child of his own to be his heir. So God told Abram he would have a child; he would have descendants like the stars of heaven and a fantastic blessing would come through him. It was pure promise. Abram's only involvement was "I believe you."

Then God told him to take a heifer, a goat, a ram, a turtle dove and a pigeon and prepare them. These were killed, as was the method of shedding blood to ratify an agreement. According to Oriental custom, when two men made an agreement they would take a lamb or a she-goat, split it down the middle, separate and lay out the pieces and then together walk between the pieces. By walking between the bloody pieces they were making a visible ratification of their covenant.

In Genesis 15:12 we read that after he had prepared the animals, a deep sleep fell on Abram. And then, when it was dark, a smoking furnace and a burning lamp passed between the slaughtered pieces. The burning lamp and smoking furnace represent the presence of God. Only *God* passed between the pieces, not Abram. It was an agreement *between God and God.* God bound *Himself to His own* covenant and once it was legally ratified by blood it could never be set aside, it could never be added to.

In verse 15 Paul says even a man's covenant, when it is confirmed, cannot be annulled or added to. The implication is that if this is true for a man-made covenant, how much more true is it when God makes and confirms a covenant. The law cannot come in and annul the promise because the promise was confirmed by God alone and no one can change it.

In verse 16 Paul stresses that the irrevocability of God's promise is all the more evident when we see that it relates directly to Christ. He is the "seed" that fulfills it. The one and only heir of everything, the heir of every promise of God, is Christ (see Col. 1:16-19). When God told Abraham his *seed* would be the key to blessing he was talking about Christ—the only way any man can ever enter into the blessing.

But what about the Old Testament saints? Were they "in Christ"? Yes, in the sense that when Jesus died on the cross, He bore also the sins of Moses, Abraham, and everybody in the Old Testament. He gathered the sins of all those who lived before as well as after the cross. All of history is included. When the blood of Jesus Christ was shed it covered sin on both sides of the cross. So Paul says the Abrahamic covenant resolves itself in Christ, the single, all important seed, through which God's promise would be kept.

In verse 17 Paul continues to argue that not even the law can alter the promise of God, because the promise came before the law and was resolved after it in Christ. God has been saving men on the basis of faith. Salvation always has been and always will be, by faith.

Paul clinches this part of his argument in verse 18 by simply saying that if an inheritance "is based on law, it is no longer based on a promise." Salvation cannot be by faith *and* by works. Paul has established that salvation in all its fullness, the entire inheritance—everything—came to Abraham by promise. If the promise is complete in itself, then it is impossible to bring the law into the situation. Either we are going to be justified by the promise through faith or by works under the law, not both.

The Galatians have to choose, and Paul tells them to choose the way God chose when He justified Abraham by faith. To Abraham God said, "I will . . . I will . . . I will . . . . " To Moses He said, "Thou shalt . . . thou shalt . . . thou shalt . . . " There is a *big* difference. The promise talks about God's plan, God's grace, God's initiative and God's sovereignty. The law talks about man's duty, man's works, man's responsibility, man's behavior, man's obedience. The promise stood for grace and had only to be believed. The law stood for works and had to be obeyed. Only one—the promise—can save.

6
THE LAW: WHAT USE IS IT?

Galatians 3:19-29

So far in his letter to the Galatians Paul has been doing his best to refute any ideas of salvation by works or justification by some combination of faith, plus works. Now he turns to an interesting question: If the law does not change the promise given to Abraham . . . if the law does not add anything to that original covenant of faith, then *of what use is the law at all?*

In Galatians 3:19-29 Paul will answer by pointing out the inferiority of the law, the purpose of the law, and what it means to be "in Christ."

Why the Law Was Inferior

Why the Law, then? It was added because of transgressions, having been ordained through angels by the agency of a mediator, until the seed should come to whom

the promise had been made. Now a mediator is not for one
party only; whereas God is only one. Is the Law then
contrary to the promises of God? May it never be! For if a
law had been given which was able to impart life, then
righteousness would indeed have been based on law. But
the Scripture has shut up all men under sin, that the
promise of faith in Jesus Christ might be given to those who
believe. (Gal. 3:19-22)

Paul begins his reasoning on the purpose for the law by
pointing out that the law was given because of man's transgressions. The *New English Bible* puts it: "to make
wrongdoing a legal offense." The law was given to show
man that he was *willfully* in rebellion against the holiness
of God. He knew he was a sinner. Conscience would tell
him that. What he needed to know was that such sinning
was absolute violation of the very law of Almighty God.

The law was given to bring about an awakened sense
of guilt before God as judge. Christ is the "seed" referred
to in verse 19. The law's purpose was to point people to
their need of the Saviour, Christ, who would come as the
Deliverer. Therefore its purpose was only temporary,
until Jesus Christ came.

Through the history of the church people like the Judaizers have been twisting things around. Satan would like to
have us try to prove ourselves holy by the very law that
God gave to prove us to be sinners! But the law isn't like a
ladder or an elevator or some other device to raise ourselves up. It's like a mirror. You look in it and you see
you've got a blemish, a defect, a problem. The mirror
doesn't have a thing to do with your problem except to
prove that you have it.

The phrase, "having been ordained through angels by
agency of a mediator," tells us more about why the law
was inferior to the promise. God did not give the law to

the people directly. He gave it to angels . . . then to Moses . . . and finally to the people (see Acts 7:52,53; Heb. 2:1-3). But God dealt with Abraham directly, even calling him friend.

The law came thirdhand; the promise came firsthand. Paul is cautioning the Galatians to not allow the law, given through two mediators, to replace the promise of God's blessed personal gift, given directly to Abraham.

That's why Paul goes on to say, "A mediator is not for one party only; whereas God is only one" (v. 20). A mediator is not needed if only one person is involved. Somebody is required to mediate only when there are two parties concerned.

Now what this seems to mean is that since the law had mediators—angels and Moses—it was a two-sided agreement. God says, "I'll do this if you'll do this." That was the character of the law. Any legal agreement through a mediator demands that both sides keep the deal. That is the position of those who put their trust in the law. They have to keep the whole law in order to be blessed.

Paul adds one more reason the law is inferior; it really can't accomplish anything to help fulfill God's promise. "Is the law then contrary to the promise of God?" (v. 21). Paul answers his own question with the same strong Greek negative term he used back in chapter 1: "No! No! No!" he says. The law and faith have different functions. If any part of the law could give life, our righteousness—our justification—would depend on the law. What the law *has* done is to put all men in jail, so to speak (v. 22). We have been arrested and can't even get out on bail. But we *can* gain full pardon. All we have to do is have faith in Christ, the fulfillment of God's promise to those who believe.

The Real Purpose of the Law

But before faith came, we were kept in custody under

*the law, being shut up to the faith which was later to be
revealed. Therefore the Law has become our tutor to lead
us to Christ, that we may be justified by faith. (Gal.
3:23,24)*

Up to now, Paul has been talking about history. Now,
in verse 23, he personalizes the historical. He introduces
the personal pronoun "we" to bring it all right down to the
experience of individual men.

The "we" here is, first of all, a Jewish "we." He is saying, "For centuries, we Jews were under the law until
Christ was finally revealed." That is the historical setting,
but beyond that, in a very real sense, it has to be broad-
ened to include a general Christian "we." Before we put
faith in Jesus Christ, we too were slaves to God's law.
Even if we did not acknowledge God's law, we were condemned by it. We were in bondage to God's law whether
we knew the written law or not.

There is no man in the world who exists apart from the
law of God. For some the law of God is written on paper or
in stone. For others the law of God is written in the conscience. But every man is subject to that law. When a man
comes to that place in his life where he knows he is in violation of that law and without escape, he is ready to be
introduced to Christ.

A young man came up to me after a Sunday service and
said he wanted to talk about what I had said in my sermon.
As we chatted, it became obvious he was not a Christian.
So I shifted the conversation to talking about the gospel.
But as we talked, here were his answers to everything I
said: "I'm not ready for that . . . I don't think I can believe
that . . . I don't feel the need for that . . . I feel that I'm
fine just like I am."

Finally I said, "I'm sorry, but we can't help you. We
can't do a thing for you here until you feel wretched and in

despair." The young fellow gave me a quizzical look, because he really didn't know how to take my remark. But it was true. As he himself had said, "I'm not ready for that." He was not ready to receive the gospel.

I am glad God made some rules that I could understand and gave me a conscience that reacts when I violate those rules, or I should be on the way to hell and never know it. Some years ago I was playing college football and I hurt my knee in practice. I should have stayed out of the next game, but it was an important one, and I wanted to play. So I went to the doctor and got some cortisone shots in the knee, plus a couple of bottles of ethyl chloride to spray on the injury during the game. With my knee "frozen" by the ethyl chloride, I played the entire game without any pain. After the game I felt great—at first. Later I discovered that I had torn up the inside of my knee and damaged it permanently. I still have a weak knee today because I rejected God's built-in system to warn me about physical injury.

In a sense, this is what God gives us in our conscience. It is a preventative, a warning system, to tell us we are going wrong.

In verse 23 Paul uses two similes to describe the law. First, the law is like a prison. The Greek says we were "in custody" of the law—guarded in protective custody. This word was used to speak of a city sealed off to keep the enemy out and the inhabitants in.

And so the law captured us. There was no escape. There was no way to get free, no way to break out.

Second, verse 23 says we're "shut up." The Greek literally means hemmed in, or cooped up.

Both of these verbs emphasize that God's law and commandments kept men in prison with no escape. We were all on death row, waiting for God to offer a pardon, which would come through "the faith which was later to be revealed." That pardon would come through having faith in the Messiah—Jesus Christ.

In verse 24, Paul uses another picturesque word to describe the law—*paidagogos*. Some versions translate this as "schoolmaster," others use "tutor." In Greek culture, the *paidagogos* was not the teacher; he was the guardian of young boys. Usually he was a slave whose duty it was to teach them obedience and self-discipline, often while accompanying them to school each day. He was the disciplinarian, which is a very important point. The *paidagogos* carried a rod and used it when the boys did not conform and this is exactly the role of the law. It is a *paidagogos,* to discipline us and ready our hearts to accept the freedom in the gospel of faith.

Undoubtedly any boy would want to grow up and be rid of his *paidagogos*. He wanted to experience freedom. This pictures what the law is to us. It is to create in us a desire for the freedom which comes through the gospel of faith.

There is another beautiful concept here. One duty of the *paidagogos* was to take the young boys to school. In similar fashion, Paul says, the law delivers us to the master teacher—Jesus Christ—so we might be justified. The law was never intended to save anyone; it was intended to deliver people to the One who could save them. Look at the Old Testament law: the rites, rituals and routines, the sacrifices, offerings and feasts. All of these are pictures of Christ. The ceremonial law is not a saviour, but it is important.

In *Pilgrim's Progress* John Bunyan speaks of Pilgrim standing out in back of his home. He is dressed in rags and has a great burden on his back. He is reading a book (which represents the law of God). As he reads, he lets out a great cry of anguish, "What shall I do?"

At this point another character enters—Evangelist—who says to the man: "Do you see yonder light? And just beyond the light, the little wicker gate and just beyond the gate, a hill, and on top of the hill, a cross? If you can get to the cross, your burden will be rolled away. You will find light and life and salvation."

And that was what set Pilgrim on his journey—his progress toward the cross. He was exposed to the law of God and realized he was in despair. The law pointed him toward the answer—the cross of Christ.

This was Bunyan's allegorical way of saying that the law is a *signpost*, pointing the way to Jesus, the only Saviour.

What It Means to Be "In Christ"

But now that faith has come, we are no longer under a tutor. For you are all sons of God through faith in Christ Jesus. For all of you who were baptized into Christ have clothed yourselves with Christ. There is neither Jew nor Greek, there is neither slave nor free man, there is neither male nor female; for you are all one in Christ Jesus. And if you belong to Christ, then you are Abraham's offspring, heirs according to promise. (Gal. 3:25-29)

Verse 25 is a transition. It takes us from one side, under law, to the other side, in Christ. The simplest definition of a Christian is "one who is in Christ." You can imagine following the teachings of Buddha, Confucius or Mohammed, but can you imagine anybody saying "I'm in Confucius," or "I'm in Buddha," or "I'm in Mohammed"?

There is no such thing as a Christian who is not in Christ. We are not following the teachings of a man, we are in union with God Himself. We are "all sons of God through faith" (v. 26). We are all "baptized into Christ" (v. 27). We are one with Him.

Water baptism is not in view in verse 27. Paul is talking about being placed into Christ, immersed in Christ. It is a spiritual, not a physical, concept. We are united with Christ in His death and in His resurrection by the miracle of salvation (see also Rom. 6:1-10 and 1 Cor. 6:17).

When God looks at the believer, whom does He see? Christ. In verse 27, "clothed yourselves with Christ," might be a reference to a Roman custom of Paul's day. A very significant ceremony in the life of a Roman youth took place when he received the *toga virilis*—the toga of manhood as opposed to a child's garment. The young man was robed with the *toga virilis,* which signified that he was now an adult and had full citizenship, with all the rights and responsibilities that came with it. He was no longer to be treated as a child.

Paul says we have been through a spiritual *toga virilis* ceremony and have put on Jesus Christ; we are robed with Him. The Christian joined to Christ, baptized into His death and resurrection, in union with Him, is clothed with Christ's own righteousness.

In verse 28, Paul moves to a revolutionary thought for his day. To be in Christ also means you are one with everybody else who is in Christ. Paul says there is no distinction, no class or racial barriers. "There is neither Jew nor Greek . . . slave nor free man . . . male nor female . . . all are one in Christ Jesus."

Why did Paul pick these three comparisons? Because it was here that discrimination and inequality were prevalent. The Jews had a prayer that went like this: "I thank God that thou hast not made me a Gentile, a slave or a woman." Paul takes a potshot at that prayer, hitting right at the three points of prejudice.

There is no place in Christ for racial prejudice. In Acts 13:1 we find that the pastors of the church of Antioch are listed. "Simeon who was called Niger" indicates the possibility that he was black. In Acts 16:1, we learn that Timothy, Paul's protégé, was the child of a mixed marriage.

There is no place in Christ for class discrimination. James 2:1-9 teaches plainly, if we are social climbers and do more for the wealthy and less for the poor, we commit sin.

There is no sexual distinction either. Christianity elevated women to a place they had never known in the ancient world. Spiritually they are equal with men. The pattern for the church and the home is to give the man the responsibility of leadership and require the woman to be submissive (see Eph. 5:21-33). But in the spiritual dimension men and women are "in Christ" and equally the recipients of all spiritual blessing.

Paul adds one more important thought in verse 29. All those in Christ are "heirs according to promise." The promise was given to Abraham and fulfilled in his seed, Christ (see Gal. 3:16). As we enter into Christ, the promise to Abraham becomes ours. In a spiritual sense we become Abraham's seed.

Everything is given to Christ. He i the Seed to whom all the promise is made. And because we are in Him, we too, receive all the promise. The moment we believed we were robed in Jesus Christ, clothed with Him. And so God can pour out everything on him because He is pouring it out on Christ.

Thomas Lawrence, British scholar, soldier and author, became known as Lawrence of Arabia. He was one of the great heroes of World War I and was a leader at the Paris peace talks in 1919. Lawrence helped represent a number of tribes from the Arabian desert and several Arab leaders came to Paris with him for the talks. They stayed in a plush modern hotel which impressed the Arabs a great deal, especially the large water faucets on the bathtubs. To the Arabs these tubs seemed to have an unending supply of water—a supreme luxury for people who had spent their lives in the blazing desert.

As the talks came to a close and everyone prepared to leave, Lawrence heard that the Arabs had secured wrenches and were taking the bathtub faucets off the wall! When he asked why, they explained they were going to take the faucets back to the deserts so they could continue enjoying the unending supply of water.

Lawrence had to talk fast to convince them that the faucets were not enough. The faucets had to be connected to a pipe, which was connected to a water main, which was connected to a reservoir, which got its supply from springs, rivers or wells. The faucets had to be connected to the *source*.

There is no blessing for any man unless he is connected to the source of the blessing. All blessing comes from the Father to the Son. When you are connected to the Son there is an unending supply of blessing!

7
IT IS HARD TO STAY GROWN UP

Galatians 4:1-20

As we move into chapter 4 of Galatians, we see Paul is still dealing with "the before and after" of the Christian life. To make his point he uses the analogy of human physical growth. He contrasts an infant son with a mature son who has passed into adulthood. A person under the law, says Paul, is like an infant son, and a person under grace, saved by faith, is like a mature son.

Paul's analogy of growth was a potent one for his readers. In the ancient world the process of growing up was much more definite than it is today. In the Jewish world when a boy passed his twelfth birthday his father would take him to the synagogue. There he became *bar mitzvah*—a son of the law.

In his childhood the law was administered through the father who was responsible for the son. When the son became bar mitzvah, the responsibility for obedience to the law of God became his own.

In Greece the situation was similar. The boy was under the father's care for the early years of his life. By the time he reached eighteen years of age he became a sort of cadet of the state and for two years was under some direction by the government. Just prior to becoming a cadet, he was recognized as a mature young man. His long hair was cut off and offered to the gods as the sign of his maturing. Once again there was a very clear, definite line between childhood and adulthood.

The Roman custom was also similar. Somewhere between fourteen and seventeen the boy would turn in his *toga pretexta* and be granted *liberalia*—he would be liberated. Having become a mature son, he was taken to the forum and introduced into public life.

No Longer Slaves, But Sons!

Now I say, as long as the heir is a child, he does not differ at all from a slave although he is owner of everything, but he is under guardians and managers until the date set by the father. So also we, while we were children, were held in bondage under the elemental things of the world. But when the fulness of the time came, God sent forth His Son, born of a woman, born under the Law, in order that He might redeem those who were under the Law, that we might receive the adoption as sons. And because you are sons, God has sent forth the Spirit of His Son into our hearts, crying, "Abba! Father!" Therefore you are no longer a slave, but a son; and if a son, then an heir through God. (Gal. 4:1-7)

To help us understand verses 1-3, imagine a child who is the heir to a massive estate. One day it will be his. In fact, he is already his by promise. But in experience he is just a child. You do not turn an estate over to a child. He may be the legal heir; he may be the master and the owner of everything; it may already be his by right if his father has died. But the child is no better than a servant. He has to take orders, not give them. He is heir by right but not heir in fact.

In ancient times, the family would assign certain slaves (called guardians or stewards) to take care of such a child (see v. 2). The child would take orders, just as any slave does. In fact he took orders from slaves until "the date set by the father." And each father had the right to fix the specific day when the child became a mature son. When that day came, he ceased being under the power of those tutors and governors and was declared mature, ready to inherit what was his.

There is an historical perspective in verse 3. Paul is saying that before Christ came into the world, Jews were under the guardianship of the written law. Gentiles were also under the guardianship of the law of conscience. So all men were like children. There was a potential inheritance; there was a coming salvation; there was an available promise; but they were not yet mature sons who could inherit it.

This is true also of any person today who is living without Jesus Christ. He is living subject to God's law. He is an infant subject to that law and the only thing that will make him a mature son able to receive the promised inheritance is to come in faith to Christ.

Notice the little phrase "the elemental things of the world," in verse 3. The definition of this phrase is difficult. Some say it means demon spirits. Some say it refers to stars and astrology. Others believe it refers to the ABC's of human religion, and that seems the most reasonable interpretation (see Col. 2:8). We are safest to let the phrase refer to the elementary teachings of human religion—rules and regulations used by both Jews and Gentiles to achieve salvation by works. Men are in bondage to these until Christ frees them.

In verses 4 and 5 we move from preparing for sonship to its realization. Just as a father set the time for his child to become a mature son, so God did the same. Paul says that "when the fulness of time came, God sent forth His Son." When the law had accomplished what God wanted it to accomplish, Christ came.

In many ways the time was truly right. The time was right *religiously* for the coming of the Messiah. After the Babylonian captivity Ezra had put together all the scrolls, and so the Jews possessed the Word of the Old Testament. After the Babylonian captivity synagogues came into use. Thus there were places where Jews were gathered in all the cities around that part of the world—a perfect setting for the presentation of the gospel.

The time was right *culturally*. Alexander had made it a Greek world and Greek was spoken everywhere, providing a common language. The gospel could easily be preached in a brief period of time without struggling over language barriers.

And the time was right *politically*. Rome had taken over the world and instituted the Pax Romana—the Roman peace—securing the possibility of free movement with the gospel. In addition, the Romans had built wonderful roads—convenient for the missionaries to travel on. It was God's time, the time for the infant sons under the law to become mature sons in Christ!

When Paul refers to Jesus as God's "Son" (v. 4), he is not talking about Christ's essence, His nature as God. Paul is referring to His role of submission in incarnation. Jesus was subject to the Father when He came to earth and submitted Himself for the purpose of redeeming us (see Heb. 1:5).

But He was not only God who took the form of a Son in submission. He was man, "born of a woman." He was fully human. In order for Jesus to save us He had to be God *and* man.

In order to have the power to deliver us out of the realm of darkness; in order to have the power to smash Satan; in order to have the power to dominate death; in order to have the power to bring God's kingdom—He had to be God. But, He had to be man too, because it was man who sinned and it was man who had to render his life as a sacrifice. He had to be God to have the power of salvation, but He had to be man to have the privilege of substitution.

Then, He was "born under the law." He was responsible to God's law. He was a Jew, responsible to the written revelation. And He satisfied the law's demand to perfection. The deity of Christ, the humanity of Christ and the perfect righteousness of Christ qualified Him to redeem us. Consequently, He was able to redeem them that were "under the Law" (v. 5).

The word *redeem* is beautiful. It paints the picture of a man going into a slave market, bargaining with the dealers, buying the slave, taking him out of the market and setting him free. Jesus set us free from the law "that we might receive the adoption of sons," and have all the privileges of divine inheritance.

Paul writes in verse 6: "And because you are sons, God has sent forth the Spirit of His Son into our hearts, crying, 'Abba! Father!' " What a thrilling reality! God gives us His Spirit. As part of sonship we have the Holy Spirit.

You are saved when you believe in Christ. That stands as an objective fact. The subjective experience that goes with it is that the Spirit enters into you and testifies to you that this is true. Paul puts it this way in Romans 8:16, "The Spirit Himself bears witness with our spirit that we are children of God." In other words, the very fact that you feel related to God and that you can cry out to God with a sense of intimacy as to a father who loves you is proof positive that you are His child.

In Aramaic *abba* is a diminutive form, used as an expression of endearment. Because Jesus had used it in His vocabulary, it passed into use in the early church. Christians would address God as "Abba Father." This is like saying "Daddy." God is not some distant person. God is "Daddy" in the most intimate sense of the term.

God sent the Son that we might receive the *status* of sonship. God sent the Spirit that we might confidently know the *experience* of that sonship. The confirmation of sonship is the indwelling Spirit.

God sent the Spirit into your heart—the Spirit lives in *you!* You have *internal power.* But a person under the law has only an external authority. He has no internal power. External rules can't change your heart. The demands might be there, but you just can't do it.

I used to try to run the 100-yard dash in college. I knew what the world's record was. I knew what the school record was. But no matter how hard I tried, I couldn't get my legs moving fast enough to break any records. In fact, I had all I could do to keep from finishing last!

I had no question about what the 100-yard dash required; I just couldn't deliver.

Galatians 4:7 speaks of the ultimate benefit of sonship—being "an heir of God through Christ" *(KJV)*. Christ receives everything, and through Christ we receive everything also (see Rom. 8:17). Through His Son God provided us with freedom from sin and the law. Through the Spirit God provided power to receive and respond to the inheritance that is ours in Christ. In making us sons, He has made us eternally rich.

So Why Are You Giving Up Your Sonship?

However at that time, when you did not know God, you were slaves to those which by nature are no gods. But now that you have come to know God, or rather to be known by God, how is it that you turn back again to the weak and worthless elemental things, to which you desire to be enslaved all over again? You observe days and months and seasons and years. I fear for you, that perhaps I have labored over you in vain (Gal. 4:8-11)

In verse 8 Paul looks back to the time the Galatians were pagans. They didn't know God; they worshiped objects that weren't gods at all.

A few years ago my wife Patricia and I visited Hawaii and toured a Buddhist temple in Honolulu. We saw the gigantic golden Buddha, with all kinds of other ghastly-looking smaller idols. Incense was burning everywhere and there were quite a few people—adults and one little girl—bowing down and going through various rituals. I walked to the back of the giant Buddha statue and there was a lady on the ground, bouncing rocks. She would bounce them, see where they pointed, and bounce them again.

And I thought to myself, "Lady, there's nobody home. Somebody made this great big potbellied thing and you're down there on the ground going through all that. But there's nobody there."

As we left that temple my heart almost broke thinking about those people in bondage to paganism, going through works and rituals to gain salvation.

The Galatians had also worshiped gods where there was nobody home. Christ had changed all that. He had brought them all the way to sonship, all the way to freedom. And now they were willing to trade it all for bondage of a different kind, but bondage nonetheless.

In verse 9 Paul says in essence, "After you have known God, how can you do this? How can you return to the weak and beggarly elements? It seems impossible!" This is progress in reverse. The Galatians are going backwards—back to powerlessness, back to poverty, back to the dreary routine of external formalism, such as observing sabbaths, new moons and all the other festivals (compare v. 10 with Col. 2:16,17).

Paul is disgusted. He wants the Galatians to get back to the simplicity that is in Christ. In verse 11 his heart almost breaks. Perhaps all his work has been in vain. Perhaps the Galatians are not even saved. Paul cannot understand somebody exchanging maturity for infancy, freedom for bondage.

In his post-graduate days at Oxford, John Wesley, son of a clergyman and a clergyman himself, was *very* orthodox. He was very religious, upright in his conduct and full of good works. John and his friends visited prisons, provided slum children with food, clothes and even education. They observed Saturday as the Sabbath, as well as Sunday. They took Communion, gave alms, searched the Scriptures, fasted and prayed.

But they were bound in the fetters of their own religious effort. They were trusting in themselves instead of Christ. A few years later, Wesley came to know and trust Christ. Looking back on his Oxford days of good works he said, "I had even then the faith of a servant, not of a son."

If we are Christians we need to remember our freedom. We must remember we are mature sons and not put ourselves back under the tutelage of the law. If we have been trying to earn the favor of God, we are infants. If we accept the free gift of God, we are mature sons.

Paul Adds a Personal Touch
I beg of you, brethren, become as I am, for I also have

*become as you are. You have done me no wrong; but you
know that it was because of a bodily illness that I preached
the gospel to you the first time; and that which was a trial
to you in my bodily condition you did not despise or loathe,
but you received me as an angel of God, as Christ Jesus
Himself. Where then is that sense of blessing you had? For
I bear you witness, that if possible, you would have plucked
out your eyes and given them to me. Have I therefore
become your enemy by telling you the truth? They eagerly
seek you, not commendably, but they wish to shut you out,
in order that you may seek them. But it is good always to
be eagerly sought in a commendable manner, and not only
when I am present with you. My children, with whom I am
again in labor until Christ is formed in you—but I could
wish to be present with you now and to change my tone, for
I am perplexed about you. (Gal. 4:12-20)*

Up to this point Paul has been handling the Galatian
problem with an approach that seems to be all head and
very little heart. He has shown tremendous conviction,
intellectual power, and knowledge of the Old Testament.
But now it seems as though his cold fury has run its
course. His anger has mellowed, his frustration is gone,
and his flaming rhetoric has died out. He slips from the
doctrinal to the personal.

Galatians 4:12-20 may be the strongest words of personal affection that Paul ever used. Here there is no scrip-
tural argument or logical defense of salvation by faith, just
a tender call to his children in the faith to stick with him
and what he has taught them.

In fact in verse 12 we see that Paul *begs* the Galatians
to listen. Paul desperately wants the Galatians to be free
again, as he is free. "Become like me," says Paul, "for I
became like you, don't you remember?"

Before he met Christ Paul had been a Pharisee of the

Pharisees, a legalist of the highest order. After conversion, Paul threw out all the legalism. He had come to Galatia just as a Gentile would have come—free from the law. Paul had started the Galatians on their Christian walk unencumbered by ceremonies and ritual. And now they were turning to the Jewish law, which they had never bccn under as Gentiles. Paul is begging the Galatians to reject this satanic teaching of salvation by law and to return to the freedom they had known in Christ.

The latter part of verse 12 should be connected with verse 13. In the midst of verse 12 is an abrupt change. When Paul says, "You have done me no wrong," he is looking backwards to his first contact with the Galatians.

When Paul had arrived in Galatia and started preaching, the Jews had walked out of his services. He came back to find that he had a Gentile audience, begging him for more teaching.

Now Paul is heartbroken. He loves these people and he knows that even they have turned against him and his teaching. They have accepted the teaching of the Judaizers, and Paul is hurt.

But the hurt does not prevent Paul from being loving. He reminds them that the first time he came was not planned. He had become sick, leaving him no alternative (see v. 13).

His illness has been the cause of much discussion. The best speculation seems to indicate he may have had malaria. Whatever the disease was, it immobilized him and he had to stay there.

Because of what he says in verse 14 we might assume Paul's disease had some unpleasant symptoms. That's why he says, "That which was a trial to you in my bodily condition you did not despise or loathe . . . . " Apparently caring for Paul in his illness was a trying, unattractive task, yet the Galatians didn't reject him in any way.

The word "despise" in verse 14 means to regard as good for nothing. The word "reject" literally means to spit. "You didn't think me good for nothing, you didn't spit on me," says Paul.

Illness and physical infirmity and adversity were always regarded by Jews as representative of the punishment of God (see, for example, John 9:1,2). Gentiles also believed that sickness was the punishment of the gods (see Acts 28:4). When those Gentiles in Galatia accepted a sick Paul, they were, in effect, jumping the hurdle of their own theology. They treated him as they would have treated an angel or even the Lord Jesus Christ Himself.

In verse 15 Paul wonders what happened to that sense of blessedness the Galatians once had. They had been satisfied with grace. They had known joy through faith. They had loved Paul so much they would have "plucked out their eyes" and given them to him.

The word "plucked" means "dug out." Why does Paul say that? Perhaps he is speaking only in metaphor. In many cultures the eyes are the most prized possession. They are irreplaceable. Is he saying they would have given their most precious and irreplaceable thing if he, Paul, had needed it?

A further possible meaning is that Paul needed new eyes. They did not have glasses in those days and Paul spent his whole life pouring over Hebrew manuscripts. He could well have had serious eye problems.

In 2 Corinthians 12:7 Paul mentions his "thorn in the flesh." It was a constant problem. Some people think this "thorn" was eye disease. Malaria can attack the orbital portion of the optic nerves. It can create a loss of color, cause atrophy, render the pupil immobile and lead to blindness. If Paul did suffer from malaria, he could have had eye trouble because of it.

Whatever Paul's problem had been, the point is this:

the Galatians had loved him. Pensively Paul asks in verse 16, "Have I therefore become your enemy by telling you the truth?" The indication here is that on his first trip everything had been fine. The second time Paul came he sensed that the Judaizers were beginning to work. So he proceeded to emphasize the truth of grace. And that is when the Galatians began to turn against him.

In verses 17 and 18 Paul warns the Galatians by contrasting his love with the "friendliness" of the Judaizers. The Judaizers were "paying court" to the Galatian Christians. They were buttering them up, hoping to win them by flattery and feigned friendship. Their motive, of course, was to get the Galatians to adopt and obey Jewish laws. Through hypocrisy and deceit the Judaizers hoped to bring the Galatians under bondage to legalism. The Greek word for "shut out" (v. 17) means literally to bar the door. The Judaizers were barring the door to God's blessing.

It is good to be eagerly sought, says Paul, as long as the motive is "commendable" (v. 18). But Paul is grieved because he knows the Judaizers are up to no good—and they are getting away with it.

At this point Paul says, "You have already been born, yet I am having birth pangs again. I went through the pain to bring you to Christ, and now I endure it again to conform you to Christ" (see v. 19).

In verse 20 he hopes to come to be with them and experience joy instead of sorrow. He is perplexed, puzzled as to how to find entrance into their hearts. If he could come and be with them perhaps he could bring a change back to truth and that would change the tone of his voice.

The Galatians were saved. But due to being sidetracked by the Judaizers there was little of Christ's beauty evident in their lives. Paul's goal was to see them conformed to Christ, to "have Christ formed in them." That is what Christian means—like Christ. Paul says, "I am hurting inside until you be Christlike."

Paul had one great desire. He wanted these Christians—all Christians—to be like Christ.

8
SONS OF FREEDOM, NOT BONDAGE

Galatians 4:21-31

After becoming almost overwrought with emotion in Galatians 4:12-20, Paul gets a grip on himself to make one final argument on justification by faith. Throughout his letter Paul has been explaining that there was an old covenant of works, and now there is a new covenant of faith. In a way, however, the faith covenant is not really new because it was initially promised to Abraham (review Gal. 3:15-18).

Again and again Paul has compared the two covenants, always showing the law as absolutely opposite grace. Coexistence of the two is impossible; one cancels the other.

In this next passage—Galatians 4:21-31—Paul will make a final comparison of law and grace, and this time he will use a different kind of argument. He will use an historical event from the Old Testament and interpret it allegorically. The story involves Abraham's two sons: Isaac, born to Sarah; and Ishmael, born to Hagar. Paul uses the account to illustrate the difference between trusting in Christ and trusting in works.

A Certain Man Had Two Sons

Tell me, you who want to be under law, do you not listen to the law? For it is written that Abraham had two sons, one by the bondwoman and one by the free woman. But the son by the bondwoman was born according to the flesh, and the son by the free woman through the promise. (Gal. 4:21-23)

Paul opens with something of a play on words in verse 21. He asks those who desire to be under Mosaic law if they are fully aware of what is written in that law. Then he shifts into his story of Abraham's two sons. Paul used this particular story for a very good reason. His enemies—unbelieving Jews and the Judaizers—were counting on their heritage from Abraham to give them salvation. But Paul wants them to know it isn't so important who your father was; it's more important, allegorically speaking, who *your mother* was.

There was a great difference between Abraham's two sons. One was born of a bondmaid and the other by a freewoman (v. 22). Not only were they born of different mothers, but they were born in different ways—one "according to the flesh," the other "through the promise" (v. 23). What does Paul mean when he says the son of the bondwoman was born after the flesh; while the son of the free woman came through the promise?

If we go back to Genesis 15, we see God's clear promise to Abraham of an heir (see Gen. 15:4). That would have been all right except that both Abraham and Sarah were well past the normal age of producing offspring. No promise child was born, and eventually Sarah suggested that Abraham father a child by her maid, Hagar (see Gen. 16:2). This was bad advice.

Abraham was 86 when Hagar conceived and gave birth to a son, Ishmael. Ishmael was produced in the normal way—a child of human flesh.

Hagar and Ishmael illustrate what can be called the "flesh principle," rejecting God's promise, rejecting the way of faith and trying to fulfill the will of God on your own. When you operate according to the flesh principle you work to obtain what God gives for nothing. How foolish!

The other child, Isaac, was born supernaturally. Sarah was barren. It was a miracle that she ever conceived. She was 90 and Abraham was 100. But God gave them a child because Abraham believed (see Rom. 4:19-22).

Ishmael illustrates legalism and self-effort; Isaac illustrates faith. Ishmael was born according to nature, Isaac was born despite nature.

These two sons became the patterns for a spiritual truth. Ishmael was a son born in the natural way and he is representative of all who have experienced only natural birth, not the second birth from above (see John 3:1-8). He was born into slavery and he symbolizes those in bondage to the law.

Isaac was born in fulfillment of a promise from God as a result of Abraham's faith. Therefore Isaac represents all those who have come to God by faith. Isaac was Spirit-born, not in the same sense as Christ being conceived by the Spirit, but in the sense that the Holy Spirit carried out a divine miracle in the physical bodies of Abraham and Sarah to make his birth possible.

Paul Explains His Allegory

This contains an allegory: for these women are two

covenants, one proceeding from Mount Sinai bearing
children who are to be slaves; she is Hagar. Now this
Hagar is Mount Sinai in Arabia, and corresponds to the
present Jerusalem, for she is in slavery with her children.
But the Jerusalem above is free; she is our mother. For it is
written, "Rejoice, barren woman who does not bear; Break
forth and shout, you who are not in labor; For more are
the children of the desolate than of the one who has a
husband." (Gal. 4:24-27)

Now Paul moves into his underlying meaning of this
true piece of history familiar to any Jew. Allegory is normally not a legitimate approach to Scripture interpretation,
but here Paul writes under inspiration of the Holy Spirit
and calls the story of Abraham's two sons an "allegory" (v.
24). It is the only stated allegory in all of Scripture.

Paul says the two women involved represent two covenants, one of law and bondage, the other of grace or freedom (see vv. 24-26). Paul describes Hagar first. She was a
slave and that meant all her children were born into slavery also. She portrays the slavery covenant—sealed
through the giving of the Law at Mount Sinai. Note that
Mount Sinai was in Arabia—*outside* the Promised Land.

Expelled from the land (Gen. 21:9-21), Hagar's
descendants settled in and populated what is now Arabia.
And they became a significant segment of the Arab race,
which could never get along with the Jews (see 1 Chron.
5:10,18-22). Today's Israeli-Arab controversy actually
started in Hagar's bedroom! And the feud still goes on,
with both races claiming that Abraham is their father, and
both claiming the right to the land of Israel.

In verse 25 Paul says Hagar "corresponds to the
present Jerusalem . . . in slavery with her children." This
means Hagar is symbolic of Judaism of his time—Paul is
saying the Judaism of his day, "Jerusalem," is in bondage

to the law, trying to do God's will in the flesh. The illustration he is trying to make with his Hagar/Sarah allegory is that the Jews have enslaved themselves to Sinai's law. They are working for salvation, but they are working in vain, because Sinai is in Arabia! Allegorically speaking Sinai is not even in the Promised Land, and that means the Jews are cut off from the Land of Promise and God's salvation. Paul's allegory applies to any time and place. The sinner who seeks to be saved through the law is on a treadmill. He is a slave—in the tradition of Hagar, Ishmael, Sinai and Judaistic Jerusalem. What started with Hagar and Ishmael never changes. God gave an inheritance, but the inheritance to Ishmael was *outside* the Land of Promise. Allegorically, that means he was cut off from God's blessing.

Jesus said the same thing about the legalists: "They have their reward in full" (Matt. 6:16), and that reward is outside God's framework of salvation by grace.

In contrast to Hagar was Sarah, who represents the "Jerusalem above"—meaning true religion with heaven as its source (v. 26). This "Jerusalem above" is "our mother," offering freedom to all who take part in the new covenant.

Paul's allegorical terms are hard to follow, but what he is saying is this: Christians saved by grace are not the children of Hagar the bondwoman and legalism. Christians are the children of faith, represented by Sarah and heaven. We have come to God through faith. We believe His promise that He saves us on the basis of grace, not works.

Heaven is our figurative mother, not Mount Sinai. We were not born of Sinai. We were born from above. The miracle of the new birth sets us free. It is an act of God, activated simply by our faith.

Verse 27 quotes Isaiah 54:1, which was originally written to the exiles in Babylon, but here Paul applies it to

Sarah. The childless Sarah is a picture of the heavenly Jerusalem. The heavenly Jerusalem was empty for a long time, barren under the old covenant. But its barrenness ended when Jesus died on the cross. The ultimate fulfillment of the "Jerusalem above," heaven, is greater than the Jerusalem below, Jewish legalism.

And that is the end of the allegory: Abraham had two sons, Ishmael and Isaac, who were born of two mothers, Hagar and Sarah. They represent two covenants and are very much like two Jerusalems. Hagar, the slave, symbolizes the Old Covenant, the earthly Jerusalem, the Ishmael mentality of law and bondage. Sarah, the free woman, symbolizes the New Covenant, the heavenly Jerusalem, the Isaac mentality of grace and freedom.

How the Allegory Applies to the Galatians

And you brethren, like Isaac, are children of promise. But as at that time he who was born according to the flesh persecuted him who was born according to the Spirit, so it is now also. But what does the Scripture say? "Cast out the bondwoman and her son. For the son of the bondwoman shall not be an heir with the son of the free woman." So then, brethren, we are not children of a bondwoman, but of the free woman. (Gal. 4:28-31)

Paul's tone is very mild, yet persuasive, as he makes an application of the Hagar-Sarah allegory to the Galatians. He reminds them that, like Isaac, they are children of promise (v. 28). Paul knows that by defecting back to the law the Galatians will trade their Isaac heritage for an Ishmael heritage. They will trade the Promised Land for Arabia. They will exchange the Jerusalem that is above for the earthly Jerusalem of Jewish laws. Paul wants the Galatians to be like Isaac (Sarah's child)—children of promise. The child of promise is the one who has accepted salvation by grace. He is supernaturally conceived—a divine miracle.

Paul goes on to mention three results of being a child of promise. First, there is persecution from the legalists (see v. 29). Paul fully expects the children of Hagar (the Judaizers) to persecute the children of Sarah (believers in grace). Ishmael persecuted Isaac (see Gen. 21:9) and those who want to live like Isaac, as children of promise, can also expect persecution—in this case from the legalists.

A second result is that the child of promise becomes the heir of a priceless spiritual inheritance (see v. 30). In the Hagar-Sarah illustration, the son of the bondwoman, Ishmael, was thrown out. Isaac, son of the free woman, was the sole heir, the child of promise. In the same way, no one outside the covenant of grace, introduced through Christ, will inherit salvation from God. Like Ishmael, the legalists will be thrown out.

The Jews historically interpreted the Genesis account of God's rejection of Ishmael to mean God had rejected the Gentiles. Paul, however, uses this passage from Genesis as an allegory of God's rejection of Jews with the Ishmael mentality—legalism. Paul knew that the only way for a Jew to be like Isaac, a child of promise, was to be in Christ.

Finally, being a child of promise not only involves persecution and inheritance; it also involves an obligation. In verse 31 Paul clinches his argument with a simple statement that has tremendous implications: "So then, brethren, we are not children of a bondwoman, but of the free woman." Paul is saying the Galatians were not born out of legalism and ceremonial law. They were *born free* and they should *live free,* enjoying liberty in Christ.

What does it mean to "live free"? Paul has plenty to say about that, and he does so in the next chapter.

9
STAND FIRM . . . IN FAITH!

Galatians 5:1-12

In his letter to the Galatians Paul makes sure the issues are clearly drawn. There are only two religions in the world: the religion of human achievement (which comes in many packages and is here represented by circumcision and Mosaic legalism); and the religion of divine grace. There are no other alternatives. In the book of Galatians Paul defends the religion of divine accomplishment in three sections. In the first section (Gal. 1,2) Paul gives the *historical argument,* where he argues for grace against law on the basis of his own experience and the testimony of others.

In the second section (Gal. 3,4) Paul delivers *the theological argument* as he trains his heavy guns of logic on the differences between justification by faith and a faith-works system of legalism.

Now, in the third section of his letter (Gal. 5,6), Paul will give the *moral and practical argument* for faith in divine grace. Paul will emphasize the ministry of the Holy Spirit, because it is the Holy Spirit who makes the life of faith work. The life of faith would not work any better than life under legalism if we did not have the indwelling Holy Spirit to empower us.

Christ Set You Free, So Be Free!

It was for freedom that Christ set us free; therefore keep standing firm and do not be subject again to a yoke of slavery. (Gal. 5:1)

When Paul talks about "freedom" in verse 1 he doesn't mean freedom from literal prison bars. He is talking about a freedom that is even better than that, freedom of conscience, freedom from legalistic tyranny, freedom from the terrible frustration of struggling to keep the law when you cannot, freedom from the pressure of trying to do things that will gain God's favor. Paul speaks of the freedom of being *totally accepted by God*—and knowing it.

For Paul, freedom was more than a negative thing. It was more than not having to keep the law to be saved. Paul knew that on the positive side freedom means walking and living in the Spirit, and he will get to this a bit further on.

The literal Greek translation of the Greek in verse 1 reads: "For freedom Christ has set us free." Christ had set the Galatians *free* to enjoy freedom. The last thing He wanted was to see them put themselves behind the bars of legalism again. The reason people are put in prison is because they do not have the internal restraint to keep themselves from committing crimes. They are placed under external controls because they are not able to control themselves internally.

For Paul, the law was like the external controls of a prison. It kept believers surrounded by the walls of legalism because they did not have the internal capacity to govern themselves.

When a person becomes a Christian, it doesn't mean he is free to be a criminal. It does mean that the Christian does not need to be controlled or restrained by the "walls of the law." He is controlled by internal restraints built in by the ministry of the Holy Spirit. The rules have not changed; God's moral standards remain the same. But the person who becomes a Christian needs no external restraints. His obedience is produced internally by the Holy Spirit (see Rom. 8:1-4).

The Results of Salvation by Works

Behold I, Paul, say to you that if you receive circumcision, Christ will be of no benefit to you. And I testify again to every man who receives circumcision, that he is under obligation to keep the whole Law. You have been severed from Christ, you who are seeking to be justified by law; you have fallen from grace. For we through the Spirit, by faith, are waiting for the hope of righteousness. For in Christ Jesus neither circumcision nor uncircumcision means anything, but faith working through love. (Gal. 5:2-6)

The false doctrine of the Judaizers is the same as *any* works system. Their particular variation said that Christians had to be circumcised to be accepted by God. For Paul, circumcision symbolized the religion of human achievement, the religion of good works.

By insisting on rituals like circumcision, the Judaizers

were saying that faith in Jesus Christ was insufficient to redeem them. So Paul suggests four disastrous results of such salvation by works.

First, Christ is of "no benefit" (v. 2). If the Galatians were to accept circumcision as necessary for salvation, they would forfeit Christ (compare Rom. 11:6). These people had heard about Christ. Many of them had believed about Christ. Some of them were on the very edge of receiving Christ. Paul warns the Galatians that if they accept circumcision, they have created a contradiction.

Paul knew that it is contradictory to receive Christ, thereby acknowledging you cannot save yourself, and then turn around and be circumcised, acknowledging that you *can* help save yourself. You can't mix the two. The choice must be made between a religion of law and a religion of grace. Salvation is in Christ alone. His provision of salvation is not worth anything unless it is fully trusted.

The second result of salvation by works is that you have to obey all the law (see v. 3). If you want to live by the law you are obligated to do the whole thing (compare Jas. 2:10). If a person wants to do good works to get to God, Paul warns him to be sure he does *nothing but good works!*

A third result of the works doctrine is that you fall from grace (v. 4). Some people have read this verse and panicked. They think they can lose their salvation. But Paul isn't talking about security in Christ. He is contrasting law and grace. If you try to mix law with grace you have fallen away from grace as a *principle*. If a man believes in salvation by works he is cut off. Christ is of no benefit to him (see v. 2). Christ exists in the realm of grace, but he is living in the realm of law.

Further, it is also true that even a Christian can fall from the principle of the grace life. Grace is God's free blessing that keeps coming when you yield to the Spirit.

When you operate in the flesh you close the door to God's blessing.

When you "fall from grace," you do not lose your salvation, but you do close the door to Christian growth and God's blessing—your sanctification. But because a Christian refuses or neglects the grace of sanctification does not mean he forfeits the grace of justification. If justifying grace were forfeited every time sanctifying grace was interrupted or neglected, justifying grace would be worth nothing. Retaining salvation would then be a matter of works!

Paul lists one more result of following the false doctrine of human achievement: we lose our hope of righteousness (see v. 5). Through the Spirit we (Christians) wait for the hope of righteousness by exercising faith. We have accepted righteousness by faith. Righteousness is ours right now, and there is that full and total righteousness that will come when we see Him face-to-face (see 1 John 3:2). We have hope because of Christ, and *for no other reason*. We have hope because of our faith, not our works. That is the difference and it is a *big* difference indeed.

In verse 6, Paul says it really is no badge of merit to be circumcised or to be uncircumcised. What counts is faith that works through love.

In the Christian, love springs from the Holy Spirit and works in the light of faith. Faith works, but the working comes out of response to Christ's love; it is not done to obtain righteousness.

There was once an artist who had a lifetime dream. His dream was to sculpt a large masterpiece of multiple characters. Finally he received such a commission from a wealthy donor. The sculpture was to be placed in a great museum where it would bring the artist honor and fame. He worked and worked. Year after year he toiled at his masterpiece. Finally it was finished and ready to win the acclaim of the world.

But then he made a horrible discovery. There was no way to get it out of the room where it was built! No one was willing to pay the price of destroying the huge building in which he had worked. Everything he had done was captive in the room in which he had done it.

What a picture of the man trying to earn his way to heaven! Everything he does in this world to merit acclaim from God is going to be left in the room called this earth. He will never bring it before God, nor will there ever be any acclaim. Whatever we do by way of works will perish with this earth. Salvation is by grace!

You Were Running Well . . . Who Tripped You Up?

You were running well; who hindered you from obeying the truth? This persuasion did not come from Him who calls you. A little leaven leavens the whole lump of dough. I have confidence in you in the Lord, that you will adopt no other view; but the one who is disturbing you shall bear his judgment, whoever he is. But I, brethren, if I still preach circumcision, why am I still persecuted? Then the stumbling-block of the cross has been abolished. Would that those who are troubling you would even mutilate themselves. (Gal. 5:7-12)

Having condemned the false doctrine in verses 1-6. Paul now condemns the false teachers of that doctrine. In verses 7-12 he finds at least five things that are true of false teachers (see also Matt. 23:13-39).

First, false teachers hinder obedience to the truth (v. 7). Paul uses the metaphor of a foot race to describe what happened. The Galatian Christians had started well. They had progressed. They had been successful. They were running well, but something had happened. Now they running well, but something had happened. Now they were stumbling and staggering, even wandering off the track!

When Paul refers to "truth" in verse 7, he could mean at least one of two kinds: the truth of salvation (see 1 Pet. 1:22,23; 2 Thess. 2:10) or the truth of Christian living (2 John 4). Perhaps he meant both. False teachers were hindering the Galatians from following the truth of salvation and the truth of what is involved in living under grace.

Second, false teachers are not of God. The Lord hadn't called the Galatians into legalism. God calls men to repentance from sin and salvation in Christ. God calls men to salvation. He does not propagate faith by works. Whatever voice the Galatians were hearing, it was not God's voice.

Third, false teachers contaminate the church (v. 9). False teachers are equal to the leaven (yeast) that permeates a whole lump of dough and makes it rise. In the New Testament leaven is a symbol for permeating sin and false doctrine (see Matt. 16:6).

Just a little false doctrine can corrupt the whole church. Jude describes false teachers in similar terms: "Woe to them! For they have gone the way of Cain . . . . These men are those who are hidden reefs in your love-feasts . . . " (Jude 11,12). Men like this are following the religion of human achievement.

The fourth thing Paul says about false teachers is that they will be judged. Paul says, "I have confidence in you in the Lord, that you will adopt no other view" (v. 10). He knew that if they were truly Christ's, Satan could not get hold of them (see John 10:28-30).

But the false teachers will not be safe. He who troubles others will bear judgment, whoever he may be. The Greek word for "disturbing" means to throw into confusion. Whoever has created this chaos and confusion is going to receive punishment (see also 2 Pet. 2 and Jude 10-16).

Fifth, false teachers always persecute true teachers. Verse 11 is difficult at first but it becomes simpler if we understand that Paul was a target of twisted stories told by the Judaizers. Apparently some Judaizers had claimed that Paul still preached circumcision as a means of salvation! Where had they gotten their information?

The Judaizers had to be referring to the circumcision of Timothy, Paul's young protégé and assistant during missionary travels. The account is in Acts 16:1-3, which says Paul took Timothy and circumcised him. But for what purpose? The answer is in Acts 16:3—"because of the Jews who were in those parts." Timothy was half Jew, half Gentile. Paul knew that if Timothy purposely and willfully followed the rite of circumcision, he would be identified with Judaism. He would be all the more acceptable to the Jews and able to evangelize them more effectively. Paul circumcised Timothy because it was expedient for ministry. But Paul would never circumcise anyone for his justification and salvation.

It is likely that the Judaizers had heard about Timothy's case and were using it to claim that Paul also taught salvation by circumcision. But Paul's response is truly astute. He says, in effect, "If I am on their team why do they keep slugging me?" If Paul had been preaching salvation by circumcision the Judaizers would not have been persecuting him.

If Paul had preached salvation by circumcision, the "stumbling-block of the cross" would have been abolished (v. 11). The cross was a stumbling-block (offense) to the Jews for a very good reason. For centuries they had staked everything on the law. Now Paul comes on the scene and says, "Forget the law. Believe in Christ and His work on the cross." The cross was an offense because it wiped out the entire Mosaic system.

The cross still offends for the same reason. It obliterates all religion of human achievement. People don't like to face the fact that they stand naked before God, guilty sinners without recourse. They get offended.

Paul closes his polemic against false doctrine and false teachers with one of the most shocking statements that ever came from his lips: "Would that those who are troubling you would even mutilate themselves" (v. 12). By "mutilate" Paul refers to *castrate*, and he means exactly what he says.

One of the pagan gods of that day was Cybele. It was the practice of the priests and worshipers of Cybele to be castrated as a sign of their devotion. Paul is suggesting that the false teachers quit playing around. They should go the whole route, castrate themselves, and become full-fledged pagans!

Paul knew that if you add one thing to faith in Christ you have nothing but paganism. There are only two choices: divine grace or human achievement. Jesus illustrated this so graphically when He told the parable of the Pharisee and the publican (see Luke 18:9-14). The Pharisee did not need anything from God. He was just reporting in. On the other hand, the tax collector stood some way off. He would not lift up his eyes to heaven, but he begged God for mercy. The tax collector went home having received God's mercy and grace. The Pharisee remained locked in his efforts to achieve righteousness.

The message of Galatians is very simple. No man ever comes to God on his own merits. God's arms are open. Salvation is available by faith through grace—no other way.

10
WALK IN THE SPIRIT!

Galatians 5:13-25

Was Paul against the law completely? Did he have any use for law of any kind?

With all of Paul's arguing against law and for freedom, it's a fair question. In fact, the Judaizers had accused Paul of being anti-nomian (anti-law), because of his preaching of grace. In this next section of Galatians (5:13-25) Paul takes time to give a positive definition of Christian liberty. He also shows how Christianity is not against God's *moral law;* Christianity stands in opposition to *ceremonial law*—earning salvation through ritual and works.

The difference has been illustrated by seeing Christianity as a narrow bridge spanning a spot where two streams come together. One of the streams is crystal clear, but it has treacherous and deadly rapids. The other stream is filthy and polluted, full of quicksand.

Stream number one, so pure and sparkling, is legalism. You cannot stay afloat in it because it will smash you on its rocks and kill you. Stream number two, polluted and full of quicksand, is libertinism (disregard of all law). Fall into it and you sink in the ooze to your doom.

The Christian maintains his balance on the narrow bridge above both streams. He dare not fall into either one.

Paul Defines Christian Freedom

For you were called to freedom, brethren; only do not turn your freedom into an opportunity for the flesh, but through love serve one another. For the whole Law is fulfilled in one word, in the statement, "You shall love your neighbor as yourself." But if you bite and devour one another, take care lest you be consumed by one another. (Gal. 5:13-15)

Paul quickly establishes that Christian liberty is not freedom to indulge the flesh (see v. 13). By the "flesh" he does not mean the physical body. Rather, he means the fallen human nature, the twisted self that is prone to sin. We were not set free in Christ to do whatever our fallen nature would want.

Christian liberty is the freedom to stop being self-centered. The best illustration of this is Jesus. He was free, and yet stands as the perfect example of selfless obedience. He said His supreme desire was to please the Father. True Christian freedom is just that—to be totally liberated to do what God wants us to do and love it. Our motivation is not the stiff upper lip of duty; it is the loving service of gratitude to the One who set us free.

Exodus 21:1-6 contains a parallel that helps clarify what takes place in the Christian's life. If a man bought a Hebrew servant, the servant had to work for six years. In the seventh year his master had to liberate him.

However, if the servant were to say, "I love my master. I don't want to go free," he could choose to stay with his master for the rest of his life. The master would place the servant's earlobe against the door and pierce the ear with an awl to symbolize his willingness to remain.

There was no difference between what the servant did the first six years and what he did the rest of his life; it was all service. The only change was in the motive. His service ceased to be by external requirement and began to come from internal desire.

The spiritual connection is easy to make: a devout Jew lived all his life by the code of Moses and by the ceremonies. When he became a Christian he dropped the ceremonies, but the code of moral truth in the Old Testament never changed. The difference was that when he came to Christ *the reason for his behavior would change.* As Christians we are free to do what is right, not because we *have* to but because we *want* to.

This is why Paul goes on to quote the second Great Commandment: "You shall love your neighbor as yourself" (v. 14). The Christian is not free to ignore the law; he is free to *fulfill* it. Paul is saying he is not bound by the external forms of Judaism. He has something *inside*—the love of Christ—and it bubbles out toward his brother. Paul quotes the second Great Commandment—to love your neighbor—because it flows automatically out of the first— to love God with all your being. Love for your neighbor is an outgrowth of truly loving God.

Loving one's neighbor as oneself was not a new concept for Paul. In fact, it is found back in one of the books of the law—Leviticus 19:18. What *was* new was the power of the indwelling Christ, which makes it possible to obey this Great Commandment.

If, however, Christians use their liberty in any way

they please, the results are what Paul describes in verse 15. The whole church will fight with itself. Words like "bite" and "devour" refer primarily to animals. If we go around taking chunks out of one another we will indeed "consume one another," as do sharks or hyenas.

Christian freedom, then, does not result in disregard for God's moral law or the mistreatment of others for our own gain (see Rom. 14:1–15:6 and 1 Cor. 8). The Christian acts on the principle of love—loving his neighbor as himself. Through love he can fulfill everything the moral law was intended to accomplish, but he does it from within. Christian freedom is expressed in self-control, love for others and obedience to God's moral law. The Christian is called to freedom in Christ, to liberation from self, to serve God, and then to serve others.

The Key to Christian Freedom

But I say, walk by the Spirit, and you will not carry out the desire of the flesh. For the flesh sets its desire against the Spirit, and the Spirit against the flesh; for these are in opposition to one another, so that you may not do the things that you please. But if you are led by the Spirit, you are not under the Law (Gal. 5:16-18)

Here Paul quickly and concisely describes the key to Christian freedom—"to walk in the Spirit" (v. 16). The Greek verb for "walk" is in continuous present tense. We are to *continue to walk,* or *to keep on walking* in the Spirit. Paul speaks of a daily routine, a continual action.

By walking in the spirit "you will not carry out the desire of flesh." If you walk in the Spirit, you have God's power, energy and strength working in you. The Holy Spirit works through us and in us in a way that never violates ourselves, never violates others, and never violates God.

There are people who equate holiness with how many times you go to church, how many times a day you pray, how often you read your Bible—the externals that lead to keeping score to determine spirituality. I knew a fellow like that in college. The school offered an *optional* prayer meeting, meaning you didn't have to go if you didn't want to. It was the only opportunity available for exercising my own prerogative as a Christian, so I took it and didn't go. One day, this classmate trapped me in a hallway and said, "You're not spiritual!"

"I know that," I told him, "but how did you know?"

"Because you don't go to the optional prayer meeting!"

That was his reply. His idea of walking in the Spirit depended on where you went, not on what you were.

Carrying out Paul's command to "walk in the Spirit" is difficult. There are problems and conflicts, as any Christian well knows. The Spirit and the flesh don't get along at all (v. 17). Paul warns that walking in the Spirit automatically leads to an inner battle.

One of the first things a new Christian discovers is that life is a conflict. Although he is a "new creature" spiritually, he still bears the sin principle within his physical body. Sin is present; he is human (see Rom. 7:14-25). People who are not Christians face no trouble of this kind. There is no conflict, because the Spirit is not there to struggle against the flesh.

Notice the word "flesh" in verse 17. The word can refer to the physical body, without any theological implications (see Luke 24:39). Or, it can be used in a theological sense to refer to that part of man that becomes the beachhead to sin—the lower nature. It is a "landing field" for Satan (see Gal. 3:3). Or, it can mean human self-effort, striving to accomplish holiness on your own (see Rom. 4:1; Gal. 6:12).

Also look at the word "desire" in verse 17. The *King James Version* translates it "lust." The Greek means to "yearn strongly." The flesh is always contesting—smashing against the Spirit. But the Christian is not supposed to just sit back and watch. He is to work out his salvation with fear and trembling (see Phil. 2:12,13) to kill the deeds of the flesh.

How do you kill the flesh? The best way is to starve it to death. Don't put yourself in the place to be tempted. Don't give the flesh anything that appeals to it. Don't put yourself in a position to have the flesh—your human inclination for sin—entertained. Starve it out whenever and wherever you can.

"Walk in the Spirit" is another way to say "Live a Christlike life." To walk in the Spirit is to pattern your life after the Lord Jesus Christ. You don't do as you please; you do as would please Him!

Walking in the Spirit not only enables the Christian to control the flesh; it also keeps him from being under the law (see v. 18). To be under the law is to be unable to control the lusts of the flesh. The law cannot stop the flesh; in fact the law stirs up the flesh and reveals sin.

In *Pilgrim's Progress* a man goes into Interpreter's house and finds a large room where dust covers everything. A girl comes in with a broom and starts sweeping. Soon everyone is gagging and coughing. The only way they can stop is when someone else comes in and sprinkles water over everything.

Interpreter explains the meaning of the story like this: the parlor is the heart of a man who has never been sanctified by the sweet grace of the gospel. The dust is his original sin and inward corruptions that have defiled the man. She who began to sweep is the law. All the law could do was stir up the dust—reveal sin. The water, sprinkled to keep down the dust, was the gospel, subduing sin and making the soul clean.

The flesh—human inclination to sin—is a powerful force and the only way to conquer it is by walking in the Spirit. The Judaizers tried to conquer the flesh by keeping the law, gritting their teeth, grunting and groaning in an effort to be obedient. They reversed what Paul says in Galatians 5:18. The Judaizers walked in the flesh and were under the law. But Paul knew from personal experience that it doesn't work. He knew you could not conquer the flesh by keeping the law, because you operate only in your own strength. You lose every time.

It's important here to see the difference between being led by the Spirit and walking in the Spirit. Every Christian is led by the Spirit (see Rom. 8:14). You don't have to pray, "Holy Spirit, lead me." The Spirit is already doing that, because you are a child of God. A better prayer would be, "Lord, teach me how to follow!"

Paul Contrasts Two Life-Styles

Now the deeds of the flesh are evident, which are: immorality, impurity, sensuality, idolatry, sorcery, enmities, strife, jealousy, outbursts of anger, disputes, dissensions, factions, envyings, drunkenness, carousings, and things like these, of which I forewarn you just as I have forewarned you that those who practice such things shall not inherit the kingdom of God. But the fruit of the Spirit is love, joy, peace, patience, kindness, goodness, faithfulness, gentleness, self-control; against such things there is no law. Now those who belong to Jesus Christ have crucified the flesh with its passions and desires. If we live by the Spirit, let us also walk by the Spirit. (Gal. 5:19-25)

Paul has given the command to "walk by the Spirit" (v. 16). He has described the conflict between Spirit and flesh (see vv. 17,18). Next he will contrast these two radically different life-styles—walking in the Spirit vs. living in the flesh.

It takes most of verses 18-21 to list all the words Paul uses to describe the "deeds of the flesh." Some are obvious, gross sins, such as immorality and strife. Others, like jealousy and factions, are more subtle—the kinds of things done by ordinary "nice guys."

Some people are skilled in masking their sins of the flesh, all in the name of spirituality. Thomas Watson, a Puritan writer, described those who fake it rather aptly when he said: "When men forbear vice, they do not hate it. There is no change of heart. Sin is curbed, it is not cured. A lion may be in chains, but he is a lion still."

Sin breaks down into four categories: sexual, religious, human relationships, and relationships to objects. You can mask your vices, but the vices are still there. They give birth to deeds of the flesh. Paul gives an ominous warning in verse 21. "Those who practice such things shall not inherit the kingdom of God." Suppose a Christian slips up. Suppose he has an immoral thought, or he becomes jealous, angry, critical, etc., etc.? The Greek term for "practice" refers to something that is habitual, done over and over.

Those who habitually do these things will not inherit the kingdom. The term "kingdom of God" has reference to the completeness of salvation (see Acts 28:31). Paul is indicating that unbelievers habitually characterized by such deeds are not kingdom citizens. He is not saying that if a Christian ever does these things he is damned.

Christians sin, but they are forgiven (1 John 1:9; 2:1). Christians sin, but they are restrained from habitual uninterrupted sinning by the working of the Spirit.

In verses 22,23, we move from the multiple "deeds" of the flesh to the singular Greek term "fruit" of the Spirit.

The flesh may manifest itself in any number of works. Not everybody who is living in the flesh is doing all those things all the time. On the other hand, the Spirit produces a single fruit.

We cannot say, "I have love and joy licked, but I am having a bad time with patience and self-control." We either have all of it or none of it. The Christian life reduces itself to this: we do not generate love, joy, peace, etc., we walk by the Spirit. He does it all in us.

This is the pattern that ought to be seen in the believer. There will be times when we fail to walk in the Spirit, when we break the pattern, but Paul is emphasizing that the fruit must be a frequently visible reality in every true Christian (see John 15:1-8).

Fruit is extremely important. The Bible makes mention of fruit in 24 of the 27 books of the New Testament. Fruit is the indicator that a man is saved. Matthew 7:20 says, "By their fruits ye shall know them" *(KJV)*. God is the source of all that fruit. If we see the fruit in a life we know God is at work.

Scripture describes fruit in many ways. Hebrews 13:15 speaks about the fruit of our lips being praise. Fruit is godly deeds in Colossians 1:10. Fruit is winning people to Christ in John 4, where Jesus saw the fields ready for harvesting. The Bible presents fruit as different righteous *actions*.

Behind the "action-fruit" is "attitude-fruit." Before we ever see the product of action-fruit there must be attitude-fruit. Whatever is going on inside will produce on the outside. We cannot love alone; there has to be an object to show that love to. We cannot have joy all alone; it must be shared. Not even goodness is self-centered. All of it is attitude-fruit that produces action.

The Spirit produces attitude-fruit and the flow comes in response. Action-fruit *without* attitude-fruit is legalism and hypocrisy. To be truly fruitful requires complete dependence on the Holy Spirit. God's Holy Spirit keeps producing. It is a question of submitting ourselves to that productivity.

It's like having someone up in a fruit tree while you are down below with your basket. The fellow in the tree tells you he is going to shake the tree and you should be ready to catch some fruit in your basket. But if you're not paying attention, or have your basket upside down, you're not going to get any fruit. What you need to do, of course, is be alert, hold your basket properly and catch the fruit as it falls.

This is the way it is in the Christian life. The fruit keeps coming; the Holy Spirit keeps producing. It's only a question of where your basket is. It's a matter of submitting yourself to the productivity of the Holy Spirit.

All the manifestations of the fruit of the Spirit are in some way significant to our relationship to God, to others and to ourselves. The list given here may not necessarily be complete. Perhaps Paul could have mentioned other graces, but he chose these nine. Let's take a closer look at them.

Love

Paul speaks here of *agape,* the highest form of love. Agape love is not emotion, it is self-sacrifice. Does Romans 5:8 say, "God proved His love toward us because, while we were yet sinners, Christ had a warm feeling toward us"? No, that's *not* what it says. God proved His love "in that while we were yet sinners, Christ died [sacrificed himself] for us." God always defines biblical love in terms of self-sacrifice (see John 15:13).

We are commanded to love the way Jesus loved, to sacrifice the way He sacrificed. Ephesians 5:2 tells us to "walk in love, just as Christ also loved you." The Spirit can produce this in us. Romans 5:5 says, "The love of God has been poured out within our hearts through the *Holy Spirit* who was given to us" (italics mine).

Joy

Paul refers to heavenly joy, the joy of God passing through a Christian. The Greek word is *chara,* a term always used to refer to joy that is based on spiritual or religious factors.

Heavenly joy is based not on how funny things are or how well things are going. Heavenly joy is based on God.

In John 16:21 Jesus speaks of the woman who has pain and travail in childbirth, but later she forgets the pain because of her joy in her newborn. Let God do what He is going to do through the pain; the joy will come.

Such divine joy is defined biblically as "full joy." No one can add to it. Full joy is joy in relationship to God, the joy of Jesus given to us (see John 15:11).

Peace

This kind of peace is a tranquility of mind based on a relationship to God. Like joy it has nothing to do with circumstances. Peace is that inward calm confidence that, no matter what happens, everything between a man and God is right.

Jesus said, "These things I have spoken to you, that in Me you may have peace. In the world you have tribulation, but take courage; I have overcome the world" (John 16:33). It is not being in peaceful circumstances, but having a peaceful heart that counts. Carry a peaceful heart into difficult circumstances and the circumstances will not be able to overrule (see Phil. 4:7).

Patience

Patience refers to tolerance. The *King James Version*

calls it "longsuffering." Patience is a gentle tolerance of others, no matter how they treat us. It is often connected with mercy and is a virtue for the believer to pursue (see 2 Pet. 1:6). The source of that patience is the Holy Spirit (see Col. 1:11).

Kindness

Kindness means tenderness in view of the weakness of human personality and the depth of human need. A characteristic of God, this sympathetic gentleness does not imply weakness. It is directed toward others. David said in 2 Samuel 22:36, "Thy gentleness hath made me great" *(KJV)*. God is gentle, tender, kind toward us. This is no Milquetoast lack of conviction. Rather it is gentleness wrapped in conviction. James 3:17 says gentleness accompanies the wisdom that comes from above.

Goodness

Goodness means moral excellence, spiritual excellence. Romans 5:7 implies a difference between righteousness and goodness: "For one will hardly die for a righteous man; though perhaps for the good man someone would dare even to die" (Rom. 5:7). A righteous person could evict a widow for not paying her rent. Righteousness is following the standard. Goodness would pay the bill for her. God is both righteous and good.

In Galatians 6:10 we are commanded to be good to all men. Such goodness can only come from a divine source. God commands it and fulfills it as we move in His power (see 2 Thess. 1:11).

Faithfulness

Faithfulness means trustworthiness, loyalty, steadfastness. If we look at Acts 6:5, we find men full of faithfulness and of the Holy Spirit—they go together. First

Corinthians 4:2 says that servants of Christ should be found trustworthy.

Meekness

Meekness (translated "gentleness" in the *NASB)* is the only grace mentioned in the fruit of the Spirit that is not characteristic of God the Father, because it means "humble, submissive to the divine will." Meekness was, however, certainly a characteristic of the incarnate Son. The term can refer in a secondary way to gentleness toward men, but since that is covered under "kindness," I feel it is best to consider meekness as humility.

In the New Testament meekness is used to describe submissiveness to the will of God (see Matt. 5:5); teachableness (see Jas. 1:21); and consideration for others (see 1 Cor. 4:21).

Philippians 2:1-4 shows how humility or meekness results from the "fellowship of the Spirit." Legitimate fellowship with Him will result in His producing "humility of mind."

Temperance (Self-Control)

Temperance, or self-control, is the ability to keep yourself in check. One of many commands in Scripture is in 2 Peter 1:6 where we are instructed to add self-control to our faith. As we walk in the Spirit and He controls us, self-control is sure to be there, too.

The totality of the fruit of the Spirit is commanded of the believer, exemplified in Jesus Christ and produced by the Holy Spirit.

In verse 23 we find this phrase: "against such there is no law." The law is necessary to restrain sin only under legal conditions. It is not necessary to have anything to restrain the work of the Spirit.

In the midst of the conflict we find there is conquest.

Verse 24 says Christians "have crucified the flesh with all its passions and desires." The minute we believed in Jesus Christ our flesh was crucified with Him. That was God's part; He did it (compare Rom. 8:1-9).

Here is our part: "If we live by the Spirit, let us also walk by the Spirit" (v. 25). That seems to be a simple directive. God paid our penalty. He gave us His Spirit, the source of our continuing eternal life. We are to walk consistently and obediently in the life He has given.

11
SOW RIGHT . . . REAP WELL

Galatians 5:26–6:10

The most important issue facing Christians is holiness. Some people may think evangelism is more important. But evangelism grows out of holiness. What is truly effective in the world is the overflow of a godly life. The top priority for a Christian is holiness, and holiness is Paul's subject as he moves into Galatians chapter 6.

The most important thing for the individual Christian is holiness. The most important thing for the Body life in the church is also holiness. We must deal with sin in our own lives, and, when necessary, help others deal with it in their lives.

He's Your Brother . . . Give Him Help!

Let us not become boastful, challenging one another, envying one another. Brethren, even if a man is caught in

any trespass, you who are spiritual, restore such a one in a
spirit of gentleness; looking to yourself, lest you too be
tempted. (Gal. 5:26–6:1)

Paul faces two factions in the churches in Galatia.
There are the "spiritual" people walking in the Spirit and
living in holiness, and the "carnal" people living under the
law. And Paul sees a potential problem. The spiritual ones
could begin to feel superior to the ones who are struggling
in their carnal efforts to keep the law.

He anticipates this in Galatians 5:26 when he tells the
Galatians not to provoke or envy one another. The
stronger Christians, liberated in the Spirit, could misuse
their freedom and "lord it over" the weaker, legalistic
believers.

What Paul urges is this: "Instead of proudly looking
down on your fallen brothers, get down where they are
and help them up!"

The first thing that a fallen brother needs is to *be picked
up*. The word "caught" in Galatians 6:1 means "to take
unaware." The best interpretation is to see it as referring
to detecting another Christian in the act of sin. Paul
doesn't tell the Galatians to play detective with circum-
stantial evidence. He says a man has to be *caught*. Whatever his problem, it has to be something that is *known*, not
a rumor or speculation. The word "trespass" is not the
word normally translated "sin" or "transgression" (see,
for example, Gal. 3:19). The word used here means to
stumble, fall, or blunder. Paul isn't talking about willful sin;
he is thinking more of a slip or mistake. Some of the Gentile Christians trying to live the Jewish law in the flesh
were falling down.

The first step is that the one who has fallen must be
willing to get up. If he says he wants help, then it is up to
"you who are spiritual" to help.

And just who is "spiritual"? A spiritual man is a man who thinks like Christ, a man who is Christ-conscious, a man who fulfills the statement of Colossians 3:16 in having the "word of Christ" dwelling in him richly.

Paul always put the burden of the church on the spiritual Christians. He never gave the responsibility for anything to carnal people (see Rom. 15:1; 1 Thess. 5:14).

So the spiritual ones are to "restore" the fallen. The Greek word here means to repair or to return to a former condition. It was used to refer to the mending of nets, or of putting dislocated limbs in place. Here in verse 1 the word "restore" assumes the person had been a spiritual Christian, living in the Spirit, thinking the thoughts of Christ, and that he had fallen into carnality. There are three steps in bringing him back.

First we help him *judge* his sin, evaluate it. Then we lead him to *confess* it to God, repenting of it. Finally we encourage him to *move out,* depending on the Spirit.

This is not punishment, because the person *wants* to be picked up. This kind of discipline is restoration for the *willing* Christian.

We don't hear too much about "church discipline" today. There is a tendency to overlook carnality and even blatant immorality because, "Who are we to judge? And besides, he may cancel his pledge and leave the church."

But the New Testament says a lot about discipline. Paul told Titus, pastor of churches on the island of Crete, to "reprove with authority" (Titus 2:15). Scripture teaches the church to discipline: difficulties between brothers (Matt. 18:15-17); disorderly conduct (2 Thess. 3:6); divisiveness and false teaching (Titus 3:9-11; 1 Tim. 1:20); and gross immorality (1 Cor. 5).

In Matthew 18:15-17 we see four steps in the discipline of believers. First, we go alone to the person concerned and confront him. Second, if he does not respond, we take two or three witnesses and go to him. Third, if he still does not respond, we tell the church. The church (very likely leaders in the church) confronts him also. If he still does not respond, he is ostracized.

All of this sounds rather harsh, and even presumptuous. But the key to the whole procedure is *how it is done*.

Throughout these steps the sinning Christian is to be warned *as a brother* (see 2 Thess. 3:15). This is to be done with "a spirit of gentleness" (v. 1). In any consideration of New Testament discipline there is to be love, kindness and an eagerness to forgive and to restore.

Furthermore, we are to restore a fallen brother with *humility*—looking to ourselves lest we too "be tempted" (v. 1). We are to be honest, straightforward and, above all, fair. Helping a fallen brother is never done with an attitude that is cruel, critical, self-righteous or judgmental (see Matt. 7:1).

The Christian has the responsibility to rebuke sin. And when the person turns from that sin, he is to be restored. This is to be done in a spirit of meekness and gentleness as we remember that we can be tempted in the same area. But there is a time when such gentleness must turn to judgment, and that is when the person refuses to respond. At that point there must be discipline.

Help Others with Their Problems

Bear one another's burdens, and thus fulfill the law of Christ. For if anyone thinks he is something when he is nothing, he deceives himself. But let each one examine his own work, and then he will have reason for boasting in regard to himself alone, and not in regard to another. For each one shall bear his own load. (Gal. 6:2-5)

After picking up a sinning brother, we are to *hold him up*—help him bear his burden (v. 2). Anything that oppresses a believer spiritually, that threatens to induce him to sin or keep him sinning is a burden.

A man I knew had a pattern of committing the same sin. He came to me for help and we got his problem straightened out. He was restored. But I didn't leave him there. I promised that I would be praying for him every day and suggested that we meet to talk about his life and growth in the Spirit once or twice a week. We agreed that he would tell me each time he sinned that same way again. It was amazing how such a relationship kept him from falling back into that sin. Since he loved me and respected me, he did not want to abuse my care or break my trust by that sin. So he gained victory.

Christianity isn't a spectator sport. It isn't always enough to pick someone up. You may have to keep holding him up. Put your life up against his. Support him, pray with him, keep in close contact. Help him bear his burden.

As we help others with burdens we "fulfill the law of Christ" (v. 2). Jesus said, "A new commandment I give to you, that you love one another . . . " (John 13:34). That is the law of Christ. The law of Christ is fulfilled, then, when I love my brother enough to get involved and give him real help with his problems.

In verse 3 Paul is assuming that the reason some Christians do not stoop down and carry other people's burdens is that they think it is beneath them. They "don't have time for that"; they get caught in the trap of thinking themselves just a bit superior to people with problems. This self-deceptive attitude can turn a Christian into a big zero as far as being effective is concerned.

Feelings of superiority (pride) come from comparing ourselves with other people, rather than measuring ourselves against God's standard. That's why Paul goes on in verse 4 to say we should not compare ourselves to a poor fallen brother. Instead, we must test our own work against

God's absolute standards to see if there is reason to be satisfied. We sometimes say, "I know I have my faults, but did you see that other guy?" The other guy's faults are not our standard. We are to examine our own lives and see if they pass divine inspection. If they do, we can rejoice in our own growth or accomplishment, not in comparison to how badly someone else is doing.

In the long run, says Paul, everyone has to account for himself. That's what Paul means in verse 5, which sounds contradictory. In verse 2 we are told to bear the burdens of others. Now in verse 5 we are told that each of us must bear his own burden. The problem lies in trying to interpret Greek with English words. Paul has two different truths in mind, so he uses two terms to maintain that difference. In verse 2 the Greek word for burden means a heavy load—something too heavy for a fallen brother to handle. But in verse 5 the Greek word means a light pack. There is one burden that we cannot share with anybody. It is the burden of our responsibility when we face Christ at the judgment seat. On that day everybody has to carry his own pack. It's a light one at that, because there is no condemnation to those in Christ (see Rom. 8:1). But in this life we are to carry each other's heavy loads.

I've gone to ministers' meetings and conferences, and I've often heard, "One thing you learn, son, is that in the ministry you can't get close to anybody."

If I really believed that, I couldn't be in the ministry. I want to get close to anybody who needs help. I can't be just a preaching machine. I want to feel close to people and have them feel close to me. I want to support them and, in turn, be supported by them.

And Don't Forget to Share God's Goodness

And let the one who is taught the word share all good things with him who teaches. (Gal. 6:6)

Verse 6 is controversial. Many interpret it as saying that Paul is giving instruction to the Galatians to pay their teachers. But why, in the middle of all this, would he give a commercial for the salary of the man that teaches? It would not make sense.

Translated literally from the Greek it says, "Let him who receives instruction share with him who gives instruction in all good things." The word "share" means to have or to hold equally. It really means a common fellowship. So the learner is to have a common fellowship with him who is doing the teaching. They share all good things together. The word for "good things" is used primarily to refer to spiritual excellence (see Rom. 10:15; Heb. 9:11).

So *build up* your fallen brother. Make certain that he gets help; and make certain that he shares all good spiritual truths with his teacher—the one who helps him.

The Law You Can't Ignore

Do not be deceived, God is not mocked; for whatever a man sows, this he will also reap. For the one who sows to his own flesh shall from the flesh reap corruption, but the one who sows to the Spirit shall from the Spirit reap eternal life. And let us not lose heart in doing good, for in due time we shall reap if we do not grow weary. So then, while we have opportunity, let us do good to all men, and especially to those who are of the household of the faith. (Gal. 6:7-10)

Just as there are physical laws in the universe, man has to come to the realization that there are moral and spiritual ones.

The popular view in today's public schools and universities is that there are no absolutes, that "all truth is relative." Secular philosophers and professors agree to absolute physical laws. They are quite confident that if they drive a car into a brick wall at 100 m.p.h. the result will be disastrous. But when it comes to questions of right and wrong they choose to be more flexible. They say that moral and spiritual questions "are up to the individual" and "it depends on the situation." The result has been the new morality and the reaping of a harvest of bitterness and death through drugs, illegitimate pregnancies, abortion, alcoholism—the continual result of "doing your own thing."

But the Scripture says that we can't do our own thing. There are moral laws that are just as absolute as physical ones. They are inviolable laws; they are irrefutable laws. If God has built a world that is governed from the physical standpoint by absolute laws, then you can believe that the moral world and the spiritual world will be governed by laws just as absolute, or God would be inconsistent. Paul quotes one of these inviolable laws in verse 7: *You reap what you sow.*

This is a spiritual law that always works. It is never bypassed; it is never avoided.

Paul chooses and applies this law to the Galatians. Now his words are directed primarily at the carnal believers who show no desire to be restored. They hang on to law and ceremony, believing the Judaizers' heresy that the Christian life is a matter of legalism and self-effort. Verse 7 is a simple truth.

Paul is actually saying: "Stop! Don't continue to be deceived by the Judaizers. Don't be led astray into works and legalism."

In another sense, the principle in verse 7 could also be applied to unbelievers. It is a general principle that applies to anybody: whatever a man sows, he reaps.

Do not be deceived into thinking that a person can violate God's law. God is not mocked. The literal Greek means to turn up your nose at God. I have talked to people who have gone to the extreme in abusing their Christian freedom. They think they are free to do anything. They *are* free. God won't stop them, but they will pay the consequences.

We are violating God when we violate this law of sowing and reaping. It is a simple law. It is the law of cause and effect. What you plant is what you harvest.

One summer we planted a rather large garden in our backyard. We had corn, squash, carrots, pumpkins—plus many other vegetables. We went on a fairly long vacation and when we returned we found some kind of monstrous plant that we thought was a deformed squash. I took a second look and saw that we had a gigantic sunflower growing in the middle of the squash! We couldn't figure it out, because we had planted squash, not sunflowers. I figured it out a little later, though. A practical joker had sneaked in while we were on our trip and planted the sunflower seeds in our squash.

Having a sunflower growing in your squash isn't the biggest problem in the world. In fact we left it there and kind of enjoyed it. But it illustrates the point. What you plant in your garden is what you get. And the same holds true for what we plant in our lives. A person's character is the harvest of early habits. A child foolishly indulged, a child encouraged to think only of its own whims and wishes may be "cute and charming" while young. But that child grows up and becomes an obstinate, stubborn, sullen, self-centered, undisciplined man or woman. And that is tragic.

Verse 8 tells us there are two fields we can use for sowing. We can either sow in the field of the flesh or in the field of the Spirit. The flesh (see Chap. 9) is the contact point for sin. When we sow to the flesh we are choosing to gratify that particular contact point rather than to gratify the Spirit. The result is corruption. When we plant in the field of the flesh we are going to reap the harvest of sin. The word "corruption" means decay and death. When the person sows to the flesh he reaps death and decay.

Keep in mind that this is a general principle. The Christian who sows to the flesh will reap corruption, erosion of the joy and the peace that he has with Christ. The unsaved person who continues to sow in the flesh all his life, reaps spiritual (present) and eternal (ultimate) death.

Lord Byron, English literary genius of the eighteenth century, sowed his entire life to the flesh. He was wild, immoral, undisciplined. He knew what his harvest would be, and that's why he wrote:

> My days are in the yellow leaf;
> The flowers and fruits of love are gone;
> The worm, the canker, and the grief
> Are mine alone!

That's a terrible way to look at life or death, but Lord Byron knew the rules: you reap what you sow.

When we sow to the flesh we reap the harvest named in Galatians 5:19-21. But how do we "sow to the flesh"? By pandering to it rather than crucifying it; by holding grudges, thinking evil thoughts, seeing sinful deeds, wallowing in self-pity and by being in places where the flesh is the target.

Some Christians sow to the flesh every day and wonder why they rarely reap holiness. But holiness is the harvest of sowing to the Spirit. We do not have to sow to the flesh. We can sow to the Spirit and of the Spirit reap life everlasting. This means the same thing as being filled with the Spirit, walking by the Spirit, being dominated by the Spirit. Instead of pandering to the flesh we yield to the Holy Spirit. The result is eternal life—full and fruitful.

Here I'm seeing eternal life in a *qualitative* aspect, not

quantitative. Eternal life is a matter of quality not quantity.

Some of the most absolutely wretched, miserable people I have ever met are people with eternal life. Because of sin they have forfeited the qualitative joys and blessings and riches of their eternal life. I am not saying they forfeit eternal life. What I am saying is that they forfeit the joy and the peace and the blessing that come when one is sowing to the Spirit. This often happens to Christians who fall from living by the grace principle.

So the Christian who sows to the Spirit reaps the qualities of his new life: love, joy, peace, gentleness and the rest. The unbeliever has no capacity at all to sow to the Spirit. He receives corruption.

John Brown, the great old Puritan, said, "Many Christians are like children. They would sow and reap the same day." Some people get tired of sowing. Verse 9 is for them: they should not "lose heart in doing good."

We all fight the problem of spiritual laziness. When we speak of "doing good" this is good in its simplest sense, not just in word but in deed. And we are to pursue that good deed at any cost. I think of Paul's unbelievable commitment to follow something through. He would not quit (see 2 Tim. 4:7).

Do not grow weary. Keep at it. In God's good time we shall reap "if we faint not."

Because God's laws are inviolable, because we are to sow to the Spirit, because we are not to faint, therefore, let us keep on doing "good to all men" (v. 10).

In the Greek "while we have opportunity" literally says, "Let us have time." It is not saying to do good at the convenient opportunity. It says to do good by *looking for* opportunity. Incidentally, Paul isn't talking here in general vague terms. He wants the Galatians to do the kinds of good he has talked about: restoring sinning brothers, expressing the fruit of the Spirit. And do it unto all men—

particularly the family of God.

In summary: if you are an unbeliever, your whole life is sowing to the flesh and you are going to reap eternal death, ultimately. If you are a Christian, sow to the Spirit and you will reap bountiful blessing. This is a natural moral and spiritual law: what you sow you will reap. So keep it up—doing good to everyone.

12
IN THE CROSS OF CHRIST I GLORY

Galatians 6:11-18

The logical mind of Paul works methodically right up to the very end of his letter to the Galatians. In the final eight verses he gives a summary of everything he has said by drawing a final contrast between himself and the Judaizers.

I Care So Much I Wrote This One Myself

See with what large letters I am writing to you with my own hand. (Gal. 6:11)

Paul usually dictated his epistles to a secretary. At the end of the letter he would take the pen, write a brief conclusion and sign in his own hand. He did this to avoid possible forgeries. In the early church forging letters under the names of the apostles was common.

I feel, however, that Galatians is one letter Paul did not dictate. He wrote it entirely himself. According to Greek construction, the more correct translation in verse 11 would be "I wrote," rather than "I am writing." This would indicate that Paul is referring to his whole letter, not just tacking on a closing note.

Verse 11 translates literally: "You see with what large letters I wrote to you with my own hand." Why does Paul bother to say this? A person with poor eyesight usually has large handwriting, and Paul may have had this problem. Some commentators feel he wrote with large letters for emphasis; still others think he was treating his readers like children and rebuking their spiritual immaturity.

But there is yet another explanation for the large letters that I think has real merit. There were two styles of Greek writing during Paul's day. One was "literary uncial"—unconnected large letters—used by common folk. The other was cursive—neat and well-formed letters—used by professional scribes and scholars. Paul's scrawling "uncial" letters suggest that he was not a professional scribe. Trained in Jewish law, Paul could probably write Semitic languages with neatness and clarity. Writing Greek, however, may have been a laborious chore. But Paul painfully scratched out every letter in bold rough strokes to show the Galatians he really cared about them.

Paul Boasts Only in the Cross

Those who desire to make a good showing in the flesh try to compel you to be circumcised, simply that they may not be persecuted for the cross of Christ. For those who are circumcised do not even keep the Law themselves, but they desire to have you circumcised, that they may boast in your flesh. (Gal. 6:12,13)

Paul may have looked at his bold scrawl and seen a parable—the difference between the Judaizers and himself. The Judaizers cared only about outward appearance—"a good showing in the flesh." Paul cared first about inner realities. Perhaps he was saying he didn't really care how his letter looked. He was more concerned about what was happening to people who were being duped into the slavery of legalism after knowing the freedom of grace.

At any rate, he goes on to make one final charge against the Judaizers, saying they desire to look religious, so they force others to be. Not only were the Judaizers concerned only with outward appearance and show; they also wanted to avoid persecution by other Jews because of the cross of Christ (v. 12). The cross was a severe offense, a "stumbling-block" to the Jews (see 1 Cor. 1:23). They were offended by the idea of their Messiah dying in such a bloody, horrible way. They would attack anyone— Jew or Gentile—who preached the cross. They preached law, always avoiding the cross.

Now, many Judaizers had joined the Galatian church on false pretenses. They had superficially identified with Jesus as the Messiah. They had accepted the cross, but with reservations. They were not saved, because they did not believe in the all-sufficiency of Christ's death for salvation. But as far as unbelieving Jews were concerned, these pseudo-Christian Judaizers were genuine believers in Christ and targets for contempt. The Judaizers knew this and thought they could avoid persecution by adding the provision that you had to be circumcised in order to be saved. The Judaizers hoped to stay in the good graces of the Jewish community by preaching salvation by works— keeping the whole law.

The Judaizers were also using circumcision to cover up their own sin. They were insisting on circumcision for all uncircumcised Galatian believers. They were imposing their ceremonial legalistic system on others when they could not keep the true moral law themselves. Religious pretense is often used to cover corruption.

The Judaizers were, in fact, trying to play both ends against the middle. They wanted to sound like Christians, but they wanted to announce they were winning Jewish proselytes at the same time. The whole thing was a front. They thought everyone, including God, would assume they were godly, holy people. But Paul tears the mask of spiritual fakery from them, just as Christ did with the Pharisees (Matt. 23:1-7).

The Cross Is the Great Divide

But may it never be that I should boast, except in the cross of our Lord Jesus Christ, through which the world has been crucified to me, and I to the world. For neither is circumcision anything, nor uncircumcision, but a new creation. And those who will walk by this rule, peace and mercy be upon them, and upon the Israel of God. (Gal. 6:14-16)

Here Paul starts to bring his flaming, yet coolly rational, letter to its close as he makes the cross the "Great Divide," theologically speaking. Paul says the cross alone is our glory.

But how can Paul really say that? The cross is the cruelest instrument of execution ever devised. There is no punishment more painful, no torture more fiendish, no death more degrading. So horrible was death on the cross that Roman law forbade execution of any Roman citizen in that manner. The Jews had despised the cross as far back as Old Testament times, because of the "curse" that went with it (see Deut. 21:23). And they despise it yet today.

During the high holy days we used to let the Jewish congregation down the street from our church use our little chapel. Everything went well, until we remodeled the chapel and installed a cross at the front. Our Jewish neighbors came to prepare for their services and I'll never forget their terror when they saw that cross. Before they could have services they draped sheets all over it, to cover up what was an offense to their eyes.

Throughout history the cross has been abhorred by everyone, yet it became the symbol of Christianity. Ironically, Christians honor a torture instrument! How can this be? The world asks:

"How can Christians get so excited about the cross? Why does the Christian symbol have to be such a horrible thing?

"What effect does the death of a man 1900 years ago have on anybody living today? Wasn't it simply a case of heroic martyrdom—a great example of self-sacrifice for some kind of a cause?

"Wasn't this Jesus a sort of misguided religious patriot who got in a little too deep and got killed for His trouble?

"Why do Christians wear a cross around their necks? Why all these crosses on walls and on top of steeples? Isn't all this cross stuff a bit morbid?"

And the Christian answers this way:

"That horrible cross was used for an act of divine accomplishment that brought to men what human achievement could not.

"What happened on the cross has lasting effects for the salvation of every man in every age.

"And unless a man puts his faith in Jesus Christ, unless he has been redeemed by what Christ did on that cross, he has no chance of knowing God or salvation."

The cross tells the truth; it shows us to be sinners. If we could be saved by our own efforts, if we could be forgiven on the basis of our own good works, there would be no need for the cross.

To Paul, how a man reacts to the cross of Jesus Christ

is the single factor that determines his ultimate destiny. It is not a mythical thing; it is not simply a symbolic thing; it is not an artistic rendering; it is an historical and actual cross.

Galatians has been called the crucifixion epistle because the cross is mentioned at least four separate times. In any discussion of the true means of salvation the cross has to be at the center.

The Judaizers had come in behind Paul and taught the religion of human achievement. They were very subtle about it. They taught that you have to believe in Jesus Christ and in His work, but you must also be circumcised and keep the law.

In his final appeal to the Galatians, Paul says there are only two options. Either you glory in the flesh (v. 13) or you glory in the cross (v. 14). The religion of human achievement glories in the flesh and praises itself. To the flesh, "reason" and man's "human nobleness" make more sense than the cross. In *Christus Futuras* Lily Douglas writes: "Reason cries, 'If God were good he could not look upon the sin and misery of man and live. His heart would break.' The Christian points to the cross and says 'God's heart did break.' Reason cries, 'Born and reared in sin and pain as we are, how could we keep from sin? How could we be blamed? It is the creator who is responsible. It is God who deserves to be punished.' The Christian kneels at the foot of the cross and whispers, 'God took the responsibility and bore the punishment.' Reason cries, 'Who is God? What is God? The name stands for the unknown. Blasphemy to say we know him.' The Christian kisses the feet of the dying Christ and says, 'We must worship the majesty we see. True reason glories in the cross.' "

During a Billy Graham crusade in Australia, a Melbourne daily paper received this letter:

"After hearing Dr. Billy Graham on the air, viewing him on television, and seeing reports and letters concerning his mission, I am heartily sick of the type of religion that insists my soul and everyone else's needs saving, whatever the means. I have never felt that I was lost nor do I feel that I daily wallow in the mire of sin, although repetitious preaching insists that I do. Give me a practical religion that teaches gentleness and tolerance, that acknowledges no barriers of color or creed, that remembers the aged and teaches children goodness and not sin. If in order to save my soul I must accept such a philosophy as I have recently heard preached, I prefer to remain forever damned."

The writer had made a choice (at least when he wrote that letter). The cross didn't seem reasonable. He could not accept it.

The gospel of grace by faith alone glories in the cross of Christ, and nothing else. For the third time in his letter Paul uses the strong negative term, "May it never be" or "God forbid!" If anybody had something to glory about in the flesh it was Paul (see Phil. 3:4-6). But he refuses to glory in anything except the cross.

To "glory" in something means to give it praise, honor or worship. Paul says he will never honor anything but the cross, because the cross is the center of the religion of divine accomplishment. When Jesus hung on the cross and said, "It is finished," redemption was accomplished. He died to bring us salvation that we could never obtain ourselves, because He is holy and we are not.

We say God is holy, but do we realize what that means? It means He is without sin, without iniquity. He is perfect and the heaven He occupies is as perfect as He is. Unless we are holy as God is holy, we cannot enter heaven (see Heb. 12:14).

Does this seem unfair? Not if you are willing to admit

God is God. He runs the universe; He makes all the rules and renders judgment when they are broken (see Isa. 40:12-28).

Some people don't like the idea of God as a judge. They want a loving, accepting, understanding God who will let them come up with their own standards. They don't want to accept God's standard for becoming holy enough to get into heaven. But with heaven and salvation, God has specified the terms. We come His way, or we don't come at all.

Those who refuse to take the character of God seriously make a fundamental error. God is not a senile Santa Claus who winks at wrongdoing. He has set down moral laws and when they are broken, it is sin. God is a loving God. He wants to forgive sin, but He cannot do it arbitrarily and be true to His own character as a just and holy God. He had to deal with sin and He did. The love of God forgives us, but the justice of God crucified Jesus Christ. Jesus died on the cross and paid the penalty for sin. It was the only way (see Heb. 9:22). When we admit our sin and believe in Christ, God makes us holy. He clothes us in the righteousness of Christ (see 2 Cor. 5:21). But what gives this whole transaction meaning, is the cross of Christ. Without the cross there is nothing to agree to. God's love provides the cross—and our salvation.

Many people will say that when Christ died on the cross it was a wonderful display of God's love. They are not always willing, however, to admit that a person is totally redeemed by what happened on that cross.

But we are totally redeemed, or not redeemed at all. God loves us and He sent His Son to die for us. And it isn't simply the fact that Christ died that counts. What counts is that Christ died for us. He took our sin. He took our place. He paid our penalty (see Rom. 4:25; 1 Cor. 15:3).

No wonder, then, that Paul glories in the cross. The

cross changed Paul's life. He became crucified to the world and the world was crucified to him (see Gal. 6:14). The Greek word used for world is *cosmos*. In Scripture it refers basically to Satan's system of sin and false religion.

People today face the terrible pain of being locked in to the world's system. I often think of the words of a lady who once said, "Life must go on. I forget just why." Paul had been in the same fix, but then he and the world parted company. The whole evil system controlled by Satan stopped dominating his life. Paul knew that God was alive, that Christ was his, that the Spirit lived in his heart.

The day we put our faith in Jesus Christ, a positional separation takes place. We have an entirely new consciousness. Vanities of the world lose their appeal. We die to that whole evil system, and we are alive to God. Everything we love is in heaven (see Phil. 3:20). Our Father is there; our Saviour is there; our home is there; our reward is there. We sense the moving of God because we are alive to God.

In verse 15 Paul says being circumcised or being uncircumcised isn't the issue. What counts is being a new creation (see v. 15).

Worldly rituals like circumcision are meaningless, inconsequential, accomplishing nothing. The frustration of the self-effort system is that it is completely incapacitated by the self that is trying to make the effort. But God makes new creatures. Jesus said you must be born again (see John 3:3). Paul says circumcision never did anything for him, but Jesus made him a new creature.

Then Paul wishes peace and mercy on those who walk by God's rule of faith (see v. 16). The words "peace" and "mercy" tie up the idea of salvation. It is exciting when you become a Christian and know you are on God's side. You are His child. You have peace with Him and experience His mercy.

So we see two sides of salvation: peace is the positive; mercy is the negative. Peace is establishing the right relationship with God; mercy is God forgiving all the rest.

By "the Israel of God" (v. 16) Paul means converted Jews. True Jews are going to walk according to this principle. I believe this is really an invitation to the Judaizers to get in on salvation, to become true Jews.

A Final Word for Christ—and Grace

From now on let no one cause trouble for me, for I bear on my body the brand-marks of Jesus. The grace of our Lord Jesus Christ be with your spirit, brethren. Amen. (Gal 6:17,18)

Perhaps Paul is talking to Christians in verse 17. Perhaps he means, "I've endured so much in carrying the gospel to you—I've been attacked and beaten and stoned—don't trouble me anymore. Let this letter settle the issue, and don't let me hear any more hassles about your wandering faith."

Or perhaps he is talking to the non-Christians. Maybe to the Judaizers he is saying, "Leave me alone. Don't harass me. You are big on physical scars (circumcision). I have them—the scars of Jesus Christ, not just circumcision. Don't question my authority. Don't question my loyalty." Perhaps he made the remark to both groups.

What are the marks of the Lord Jesus? Every blow that Paul ever took as a Christian was really aimed at Jesus Christ. He had the joy of taking the punishment (see 2 Cor. 1:5; 4:10).

The world wanted to attack Jesus. They could not get to Him because He had gone, so they got to Paul instead. Any time the world persecutes a Christian they are persecuting Jesus. When you take a blow for the truth it is really meant for Jesus Christ.

Paul finishes his letter on a note of grace, the keynote of the entire epistle.

In his final line Paul prays that "the grace of our Lord Jesus Christ" will be with his brothers in the faith (v. 18). It is only fitting that Paul ends his letter by mentioning grace—the keynote of Galatians. Grace—God's unmerited favor—is what changed Paul from murderous legalist to loving servant of Christ. Grace had freed the Galatians from their bondage in sin under the law. Grace is what would keep them free in Christ.

In John Bunyan's great allegory, *Holy War*, (adapted from Ethel Barrett's *The Great Conflict*) there is a dramatic closing scene between Emmanuel (Christ) and residents of the town of Mansoul (you and me). Emmanuel has helped them beat off the Diabolonians (Satan's army) and now he stands in the town square telling them how to stay free from Satan's clutches. Emmanuel says:

"I have loved you, Mansoul. I bought you for a price; a price not of corruptible things, as of silver and gold, but a price of blood, my own blood, which I spilled freely to make you mine, and to reconcile you to my father.

"And I stood by you in your backsliding, when you were unfaithful, though you did not know I was there. It was I who made your way dark and bitter. It was I who put Mr. Godly-Fear to work. It was I who stirred up Conscience and Understanding and Will. It was I who made you seek me, and in finding me, find your own health and happiness.

"Nothing can hurt you but sin; nothing can grieve me but sin; nothing can make you fall before your foes but sin; beware of sin, my Mansoul.

"I have taught you to watch, to fight, to pray, and to make war against your foes; so now I command you to believe that my love is *constant* to you.

"O my Mansoul, how I have set my heart, my love upon you!

"Show me your love—and hold fast—until I take you to my father's kingdom where there is no more sorrow, no grief, no pain . . . .

"Where you shall never be afraid again . . . . "

As Emmanuel rides away in his chariot, Conscience, Understanding and Will discuss the future and how they will have to be alert to keep the Diabolonians at bay. Unless they depend completely on King Shaddai (the Father), Emmanuel (the Son), and the Lord High Secretary (the Holy Spirit) they will fail and fall into Enemy hands.

"Is this way better than the freedom you had before?" asks Understanding, referring back to days before Emmanuel had come into their lives.

"The freedom we had before was like—" Will struggled for words, "like birds flying through broken windows in-and-out of a deserted house—flying aimlessly, going nowhere."

"Do you love him because you have to?" Understanding's probing was gentle; their talk was to reiterate their faith, and in their talking they strengthened each other.

"I do not have to love him," said Will. "I am free. He has always left me free to do as I please."

"Then?"

"I love him because I want to," Will said simply. "And I can never love him enough."

And that is Paul's letter to the churches in a far-off land called Galatia. It is his letter to us today. *In Christ we are free.* Such freedom is priceless. Never, *never* give it up.

BIBLIOGRAPHY

I am indebted to the following commentaries for much assistance in the preparation of this book.

Barclay, William. *The Letter to the Galatians*. Philadelphia, PA: Westminster Press, 1958.

Burton, Ernest De Witt. *The International Critical Commentary: Galatians*. Edinburgh: T. & T. Clark, 1971.

Cole, R. A. *The Epistle of Paul to the Galatians*. Grand Rapids, MI: Wm. B. Eerdmans, 1970.

Hendriksen, William. *New Testament Commentary: Exposition of Galatians*. Grand Rapids, MI: Baker Book House, 1971.

Lightfoot, J.B. *The Epistle of Paul to the Galatians*. Grand Rapids, MI: Zondervan, 1962.

Ridderbos, Herman N. *The Epistle of Paul to the Churches*

of Galatia. Grand Rapids, MI: Wm. B. Eerdmans, 1953.

Stott, John R.W. *The Message of Galatians*. London: Inter-Varsity Press, 1968.

Tenney, Merrill C. *Galatians: The Charter of Christian Liberty*. Grand Rapids, MI: Wm. B. Eerdmans, 1961.

Wuest, Kenneth S. *Wuest's Word Studies Vol. I*. Grand Rapids, MI: Wm. B. Eerdmans, 1966.